One God, Many Faiths
One Garden, Many Flowers

Hushidar Hugh Motlagh, Ed.D.

Global Perspective

Mt. Pleasant, Michigan

One God, Many Faiths
One Garden, Many Flowers

ISBN 0-937661-04-X (cloth)
ISBN 0-937661-03-1 (paper)
Library of Congress Catalog Card No. 98-94041

Cover design by Lori Block.

To order copies of this book and other works by this author, in the United States call or fax:

1-800-949-1863

If you prefer, order online from any country:

www.globalperspective.org

For further information and possible change of our address, visit our Web Site or send us an email to:

info@globalperspective.org

Our present address:
Global Perspective, 1106 Greenbanks Dr. Mt. Pleasant, MI 48858, U.S.A

May 2018

Contents

Preface

Questions and Answers About the Bahá'í Faith

* * *

Preface

What Can You Gain from This Book?

We understand why children are afraid
of darkness. But why are people afraid
of light?   Plato

It takes a special person to reach for the light, to go
beyond the comfort zone of tradition and conformity.
Selecting or accepting a book of this kind puts you
at the top of the pyramid of light-lovers. It shows
a desire to discover; it points to an open mind,
unafraid to expand; it indicates courage to step
beyond the safety of the familiar and the popular;
it demonstrates a sense of trust and hope that there
is more to life than is found in the morning paper
or on the evening news.

This book is for those who wish to see the world grow up, who feel like the little girl who said, "I'd like to be six. I'm tired of being five. I have been five for the whole year!"

Many people live "lives of quiet desperation." They believe they cannot make any difference. This book undermines that belief. It shows how a small step can lead to giant leaps for you and for humankind, how a sincere desire can bring rewards beyond expectation. I hope the knowledge this book presents will help you take that small step with excitement and confidence. I hope it will stir and expand your desire for truth to blossom into an everlasting and ever-growing garden of joy and peace.

One God, Many Faiths presents the joyous news of the coming of the Kingdom, a news for which people have been waiting for thousands of years. It is written to proclaim that the Promised One of all nations and religions has come! It contains the most glorious message the human race has ever known: *that the time is ripe for the peoples of the world to become one people, under one God and under one faith*.

The age of separation has passed, the time of togetherness has come. We can survive and prosper only by cooperating and caring for each other. A lady lost power in her car at a traffic light. The young driver behind her kept honking his horn. The lady stepped out of her car, went to the young man and said, "If you come and get my car started, I will blow your horn for you."[1] The world needs people who will step out of their little comfort zone and, instead of just sitting and making noise, become a part of the divine symphony.

One God, Many Faiths is about a new Faith—the Bahá'í Faith—that is unifying the peoples of all religions under one God. The knowledge of the new Faith—its marvelous teachings and incredible history—will lead you away from the stale odor of gloom and doom to a new and splendid garden. You will be surrounded by rows and rows of fragrant flowers. From every petal of those flowers you will hear a new song and symphony of peace and oneness, of hope and harmony.

You can be certain of this: If you investigate the Bahá'í Faith with a thirsting and humble heart, you will experience a sense of spiritual fulfillment that will edify and enrich your life beyond expectation. Once you have reached the end of your journey, you will say, "How could I have lived without it?" Your degree of spiritual capacity and thirst for truth will determine the heights to which you will soar.

The purpose of this book is to share with you the greatest and most joyous news the world has ever known, the ***knowledge*** of the most glorious advent in human history.

> Through ***knowledge*** shall the just be delivered.[✤]
>
> Proverbs 11:9

> There is nothing of greater importance to man-kind than ***the investigation of truth***.[2]
>
> Bahá'í Scriptures

✤ Emphasis added to quotations from sacred scriptures throughout the book by this author.

Choosing Your Everlasting Destiny

In this age of information overload, only a few people buy books, and of those who do, according to one report, only 10 percent read beyond the first few chapters! I hope you are one of those few champions who will persist to the finish line, one of those special people who put their spiritual destiny above everything else. If some topics interest you more than others, do not hesitate to read them first. But please make every effort to cover every topic. Otherwise, you may not see the celestial scene, the grand design of your spiritual destiny. Even a small patch of cloud—a lack of knowledge—can prevent you from seeing the sun.

Deep inside us there is a feeling that nothing happens by chance. Is there a reason you heard about the Bahá'í Faith? Is an invisible hand guiding you? God is ever-present in our lives and constantly puts signs in our path, which we often fail to see.

Christ specifically asked us to pray, so that we might know Him at His return:

Take ye heed, watch and *pray*... Mark 13:33

Watch ye therefore, and *pray always*... Luke 21:36

Before embarking on this most critical and far-reaching journey of your life, pray that you will be assisted every step of the way. Will the One who asks us to pray ignore our prayers? Will He not hold our hands if we ask Him?

Whatsoever ye shall ask in prayer, believing, ye shall receive.   Christ (Matt. 21:22)

For everyone who asks receives; he who seeks finds; and to him who knocks, the door will be opened.   Christ (Matt. 7:7-8)

And everyone who calls on the name of the Lord will be saved...   Joel 2:32

This prayer should ascend from every heart, it should become everyone's daily desire:

Show me thy ways, O Lord, teach me thy paths.
Psalms 25:4-5

Through childhood training we become emotionally programmed into a specific system of belief. This system cannot be turned off and on by the sheer weight of evidence. A candle, however perfect, cannot set itself on fire. Without the light of God the soul is only a lump of wax. But as soon as it makes a move, it ignites the spark of truth, it sets in motion the heart of Heaven.

Concerning all acts of initiative and creation, there is one elementary truth—that the moment one definitely commits oneself, then Providence moves, too.   Johann Goethe

Wisdom indicates that the worthiest way to spend life is to invest it in something that outlives life, to devote it to a purpose that never dies. I hope the study of the Bahá'í Faith will serve that purpose for you. I hope you are among the few who have faith in God's promises and are dedicated to discovering the knowledge of their fulfillment. I hope you are among those who will take time to uncover this greatest of all mysteries: the coming of the One promised in all Scriptures, the supreme Messenger and Redeemer of our time, for whom the world has been waiting for thousands of years. "Actions deferred are all too often opportunities lost."

Obviously, you are not an average person. The fact that you are reading this book is evidence that you already have climbed from the deep valleys of apathy and unawareness, that you already are at the top of the pyramid of light-lovers. Let me therefore salute you for your wisdom, courage, and commitment to embarking on a journey that will continue beyond time into the eternal future. Let me commend you for giving a high priority to your spiritual life and destiny, for making an independent investigation of truth. Let me also thank you for the honor of allowing me to share with you a message that has transformed my life beyond estimation and that can transform yours and that of every other person on our planet. May your search be a step that will lead to giant leaps for you and for humankind. I cherish the hope that some day I will have the honor of meeting you and knowing you. Until then, may God bless you and assist you in all your endeavors.

Hugh Motlagh

The Promise of All Ages

The desired of all nations shall come. Haggai 2:7

On that day the Lord shall be one Lord and his name the one name.   Zechariah 14:9

And I...am about to come and gather all nations and tongues, and they will come and see my glory.   Isaiah 66:18

Soon will the present day Order be rolled up, and a new one spread out in its stead.

Bahá'í Scriptures

All nations and kindreds...will become a single nation. Religious and sectarian antagonism, the hostility of races and peoples, and differences among nations, will be eliminated.

Bahá'í Scriptures

Ye are the fruits of one tree, and the leaves of one branch. Deal ye one with another with the utmost love and harmony, with friendliness and fellowship...So powerful is the light of unity that it can illuminate the whole earth. The One true God, He Who knoweth all things, Himself testifieth to the truth of these words.

Bahá'í Scriptures

Questions and Answers About the Bahá'í Faith

He Who Seeks Finds

Ask and it will be given to you; seek and you will find; knock and the door will be opened to you. For everyone who asks receives; he who seeks finds; and to him who knocks, the door will be opened.

Christ (Matt. 7:7-8)

Call to me and I will answer you and tell you great and unsearchable things you do not know.　　　　　Jeremiah 33:3

He rewards those who earnestly seek Him.

Hebrews 11:6

Why Should Everyone Investigate the Bahá'í Faith?

God has always sent knowledge through His Messengers and Redeemers. And He has always asked us to look for them, to find them, and to follow them. Searching is always the first essential step. What did Christ mean by saying, "*Watch*!"? What did He mean by saying that He would come "like a thief"?

> That is the day when I come like a *thief*! Happy the man who stays *awake*...   Christ (Rev. 16:15)

> Be on guard! Be alert!...keep watch...do not let him find you *sleeping*. What I say to you, I say to everyone: "*Watch*!"   Christ (Mark 13:33-37)

> Be always *on the watch*...that you may be able to stand before the Son of Man.
> Christ (Luke 21:36)

What, then, did Christ mean by "Watch!"? Did He mean "Watch the evening news!" "Watch the Sunday morning sermon and choir!" "Watch political and religious leaders in debate!"? No, He meant watch for *the news of His coming!* Only a "thief"—the One people fail to see—requires careful and constant watching. And who do you think will find a "thief"? The one who dreams or the one who acts? The one who sits and waits, or the one who *looks* for Him?

> Unto them that *look for Him* [Christ] shall He appear the second time.   Hebrews 9:28

Could the instructions about the need for investigation be more clear, more emphatic? Why, then, do many people fail to follow the Word of their Master?

Not only are we asked to look for "the thief," not only are we urged to watch for *the news* of His coming, we are also asked to keep a watch on *ourselves*, so that we have the courage to investigate His message and the insight to see His divine glory and splendor. The twin "watchings"—for Him and for ourselves—are intertwined.

> *Keep a watch on yourselves*; do not let your minds be dulled by dissipation and drunkenness and worldly cares...Be on the alert...
>
> Christ (Luke 21:34-36)

Why did Christ choose such a powerful and vivid metaphor—a thief who comes in the dark of the night—to describe His return? And why did He emphasize the need for staying awake and alert? Because He knew that at His coming people would be spiritually asleep. They would not hear the alarm, they would not hear the new song, but would continue to dream in the dark of unawareness.

How would you respond if a colleague or acquaintance made this statement: "There is a religion called the Bahá'í Faith. Its followers believe that Christ has already returned. And they have 1,800 reasons to prove it"? Would you say, "Show me those reasons, where can I find them?" And if in response your friend said, "You can find them in three volumes, each about 500 pages." Would you say, "Where can I find those volumes? I can't wait to read them"? Or would you simply ignore the news? If you are an average person, you would probably ignore the news.

How did you respond to the number 1,800? Did you think it was a random number? Would you be surprised to know that the figure 1,800 is true, that the Bible does contain so many prophecies about the Bahá'í Faith? And would it surprise you to know that they all have come to pass? (You can read those prophecies in *I Shall Come Again, Lord of Lords,* and *King of Kings*.)✢

If this claim is indeed true, if all these prophecies have actually been fulfilled by the Bahá'í Faith, why are most people unaware? Does not this lack of awareness fulfill the prophecies comparing the return of Christ to the coming of a thief?

What has happened is hard to believe. How can so much evidence remain unknown? How can the greatest and most anticipated news in history remain unrecognized? How can so much glory remain concealed beyond "the clouds" of unawareness?

The One who uttered those 1,800 prophecies knew that to a sleeper no amount of evidence can make any difference. A dreamer can sleep through the most majestic and magnificent dawn without the slightest awareness. Even a little sleepiness can prevent a soul from seeing the splendor of the sun.

✢ If you are investigating the Bahá'í Faith and have a desire to read one of these Volumes, I will be honored to send you a free copy. More about this offer later in this book.

We can see how perfectly—in spite of massive evidence pointing to His return—Christ's promise and prediction of His "thief-like" advent has come to pass. We can see how the greatest news in human history has remained mostly unnoticed.

After more than a century, many still have not heard the wake up call. Many are still unaware that in the mid-19th century, when muddy waters began to rise and threaten our planet and its peoples and the old order began to shake and crumble, God sent His Ark of salvation—a new Messenger with a new Faith and a new world order for peace and unity, a Faith with practical solutions not only to our personal and spiritual life but also to our economic, social, and political problems. This book offers brief responses to some of the questions people ask frequently about this Faith—the Bahá'í Faith.

The Bahá'í Faith has a powerful and timely message that can transform your life on a scale you did not think possible. It can help you see your role on this planet in an entirely new light. It can strengthen your faith in God and inspire you to reach for new heights of awareness and spirituality. It reveals a Secret that has remained unknown for thousands of years.

> Shout and be glad...For I am coming, and I will live among you, declares the Lord.
>
> Zechariah 2:10

> This is the Day of great rejoicing. It behoveth everyone to hasten towards the court of His nearness with exceeding joy...[1] Bahá'í Scriptures

What Is the Bahá'í Faith?

Bahá'í is a new independent Faith, born in 1844. Only once in a thousand years is a great religion such as the Bahá'í Faith born. Its followers are called *Bahá'ís*, meaning "those who follow the light." The prime purpose of the Bahá'í Faith is to spiritualize humanity, to make religion relevant to our time, to restore its purity and vitality, and to focus and direct its energies toward the goal of creating a global society, a new world civilization based on justice, peace, and unity.

The Bahá'í Faith is the second most wide spread religion in the world, next to Christianity. The following figures, based on *The Britannica Book of the Year*, show the number of countries and territories to which various religions have spread:

- Christianity   254
- Bahá'í Faith   205
- Islam   172
- Hinduism   88
- Buddhism   86[2]

Bahá'í is a faith whose coming is promised in all sacred Scriptures. They have all foretold that, at a given point in history, when darkness and despair have spread, when "the great tribulation" has engulfed the human race, God will send a new light for all the peoples of the world to guide them and unite them. Bahá'ís believe that light has come. You are invited to investigate it for yourself, as have other like-minded millions. The more you pursue it, the greater your astonishment will be. You will keep saying to yourself, "This faith has been around for some 150 years. Why didn't I know about it before? It has such wonderful solutions to social and spiritual

problems of our time. Why don't more people look
into it? Why don't our religious and political leaders
adopt and apply its teachings?" If you are an open-
minded and determined seeker of truth, you will
derive such spiritual nourishment from your new
knowledge that it will astonish you. You will say
to yourself, "I had no idea I was missing so much!"

We don't know what joys we are missing until we
experience them. We don't know we have been
drunk until we become sober. Some years ago, the
editors of *Psychology Today* sent questionnaires to
their subscribers to find out what makes people
happy. One subscriber wanted to see the results of
the survey. "I think I am happy," he wrote. "Would
you please verify?"

I have had the honor and pleasure of observing
with astonishment the awakening of many seekers
of truth to new horizons of hope, happiness, and
harmony. I have witnessed dramatic and sudden
transformations in the attitudes and lives of men
and women of all backgrounds: Catholic, Protestant,
Jew, Muslim, Atheist, young, old, the sophisticated,
and the simple. You now have a chance to witness
it for yourself.

> God's wisdom is proved by its result.
>
> Christ (Matt. 11:19)

The Bahá'í teachings remove the obstacles that pre-
vent people from reaching their highest potential.
They cultivate positive and critical thinking, self-
esteem, self-actualization, and enlightened faith.
Dogmatism and blind faith have no place in the
Bahá'í Faith.

To manifest greatness, we need a great purpose. To attain oneness, we need one divine destiny. To cultivate our love, we need to connect to One we can all love.

By fostering the knowledge and love of God, the Bahá'í Faith reveals new dimensions of joy, peace, and harmony. In the light of its teachings, life glows with an enduring purpose, it rises from the depths of a depressive and monotonous cycle into an everlasting adventure of hope and fulfillment. Without a cosmic and eternal perspective, which can come only from knowing and loving God, life loses its luster, its enduring purpose and excitement.

Where there is no vision, the people perish.
Proverbs 29:18

About two centuries ago we encountered a new frontier: learning to live in a new world expanded by an explosion of knowledge, which is now doubling approximately every ten years. Then came the second frontier: controlling and guiding that explosion for the good of the world. A third frontier now presents us with a challenge greater than we have ever encountered: learning a new way of thinking about who we are, what on earth we are doing, and where we are going; learning to live with ourselves and our neighbors in this global village. The Bahá'í Faith has come to prepare us and lead us along this latest frontier, perhaps our last.

"Everyone goes to the forest. Some go for a walk to be inspired, and others go to cut down the trees." We invite you to come for an inspiring tour through a beautiful, blooming forest filled with perfumed flowers.

When Christ came, He introduced a new paradigm,
a new way of looking at things. He changed "an
eye for an eye, a tooth for a tooth" into "love your
enemies:"

> You have heard that it was said, love your neigh-
> bor and hate your enemy. But I tell you, love
> your enemies and pray for those who persecute
> you.   Christ (Matt. 5:43-44)

That was a major paradigm shift. It required a
radical change in thinking. Today the Bahá'í Faith
asks us for still another shift, one that is more far-
reaching than the one Christ proclaimed. The Bahá'í
paradigm includes the following:

- *The world should no longer be viewed as a divided
  house but as one country, and all humankind its
  equal citizens*. Our eyes are different from our
  elbows, our skin from our stomach, and our lips
  from our liver, yet we know them all as members
  of *one* body. That is how we should perceive
  the diverse races and cultures of the world. We
  must respect and appreciate one another's differences and work together in unison. "A man may
  die, nations may rise and fall, but an idea lives
  on." "Unity in diversity" is one of those immortal truths whose time has come.

We must set aside our prejudices and perceptions
of superiority and embrace the principle of oneness. A Baptist pastor got angry at his young
son for hitting his Jewish friend. He told his
son, "You should be ashamed of yourself. Don't
you know that Jesus was a Jew?" "Dad, I'm
sorry," he replied. "I know God is a Baptist, but

I didn't know that Jesus was a Jew." The age of separation and superiority is passed.

The time is ripe for unifying this fragmented and fragile planet and bringing peace to its diverse and divided peoples. As Adlai Stevenson said, "We travel together, passengers in a little space-ship, dependent on its vulnerable supplies of air and soil...preserved from annihilation only by the care, the work, and the love, we give our fragile craft."

- *We have reached the age of maturity.* We should no longer act like children who believe and do what their parents tell them. We should investigate the truth for ourselves and *choose* our faith rather than depend on *chance*—our religious leaders or our ancestors—to make our choices. Digging for evidence takes more time and effort than jumping to a conclusion, but it is a rewarding, uplifting, and stimulating experience.

- *Every individual needs an enduring purpose.* Without purpose, the joy of living turns into pain and suffering, like that of "the young man who went to a psychologist and said, 'Doc, I'm ready to end it all. I have nothing to live for anymore.' The doctor said, 'What do you mean you have nothing to live for? You haven't paid for your house. You haven't paid for your car. You haven't paid for your furniture. You haven't paid me for this visit. You've got plenty to live for!'"

Ours is the most painful period in history, yet it should be the most joyful. The Bahá'í Faith is a religion of peace and contentment, of hope and vision. It has come at the most troubled time in history to make us the happiest people who have ever lived.

Our foremost purpose in life is discovering and expressing our spiritual potential. That is the only way we can attain true contentment and fulfillment. Everything we do must serve that purpose.

- *Only the Word of God can transform the heart and inspire everlasting love, peace, and happiness.* "Our faith can make us larger than our losses, greater than our griefs, stronger than our struggles, and more powerful than our problems."

- *About once in a thousand years God sends a new Messenger or Redeemer to teach us new knowledge measured to our capacity.* The City of God has been renewed in the past and will continue to be renewed in the future.

- *The Bahá'í Faith is the glorious Gift of God for this day.* It is the blueprint for building the City of God, a world of peace and prosperity. It is Heaven's design for creating love, hope, and happiness on this divided and depressed planet. Our job is to build the City based on the blueprint.

Bahá'ís believe that, "It's better to light a small candle than to curse the darkness." They are all over this planet lighting little candles. At last the light of the new knowledge will transform our planet into a vast garden of blooming lights. Thousands of Bahá'ís have left their countries and settled where they can make a difference. They devote their lives to helping the disadvantaged and the poor. Their efforts range from raising chickens to forming women's literacy classes; from conducting health and hygiene seminars to establishing preschools for village children.

A pastor lost patience with his inactive church members. To encourage action, he read this verse from the Bible, "They brought to Jesus all sick people with diverse diseases" (Matthew 4:24). He then proceeded to interpret the verse. He said, "Sometimes you go to a doctor, he checks you, and gives you the right remedy for a quick recovery. But when you have 'Diverse Disease,' only the Lord can cure you. Dear friends, we have seen an epidemic spread of 'Diverse Disease' among our people. Some dive for the door as soon as the sermon is over. Some dive under the blanket to rest when they should be up celebrating the Lord's Day. Others dive for the TV set or into their car for a cruise. Others dive into a big bag of excuses for being too busy to take on the work of the Lord. Still others dive into a flurry of fault-finding when they should be looking at their own faults. Yes, dear friends, doctors may cure you of any disease except 'Diverse Disease.' That, only the Lord can do."

The pastor was right, there is a sickness that only God can cure: that is a "diseased soul," one out of touch with its Creator. The Bahá'í Faith has come to restore the spiritual health of humanity.

Today, many Christians acknowledge the urgent need for a paradigm shift in our thinking from provincial to planetary, from religiosity to spirituality, the need for a fresh outpouring of the spirit that transforms and expands our vision. As Matthew

Fox wrote in *The Coming of Cosmic Christ*, "It is time to move from the quest for the historical Christ to the quest for Cosmic Christ...This Cosmic Christ will...effect a change of heart, a change of culture, a change of ways...'By their fruits will you know them,' Jesus advised. A true awakening to the Cosmic Christ will effect genuine result."[3] He then asks, "Is it possible that our entire civilization is depressed because we lack the Cosmic Christ perspective?"[4] Even some secular scientists acknowledge the need for a new spiritual power. Paul Ehrlich of Stanford University declared, "Scientific analysis points, curiously, toward the need for a quasi-religious transformation of contemporary cultures."[5]

President Roosevelt had a perfect vision not only of what America needs but of what the world needs:

> No greater thing could come to our land today than a revival of the spirit of religion...a revival that would sweep through the homes of the nation...to their reassertion of their belief in God. I doubt if there is any problem, social, political or economic, that would not melt away before the fire of such a spiritual awakening.[6]

Who Are the Central Figures of the Bahá'í Faith?

The central figures of the Bahá'í Faith are the *Báb*, meaning *the Gate*; *Bahá'u'lláh*, meaning *Glory of God*; and *'Abdu'l-Bahá*, meaning *Servant of Glory*. The Báb was the Herald of Bahá'u'lláh and came to prepare the way for Him. The Báb, condemned for His claim, was executed in 1850. In 1863,

Bahá'u'lláh declared that He was the One promised by the Báb and all the great Messengers of the past. Bahá'u'lláh, the founder of the Bahá'í Faith, brought a vast store of knowledge and wrote as many as a hundred volumes. 'Abdu'l-Bahá, His son, served as a perfect example to manifest the awesome beauty and splendor of our spiritual potential and to translate Bahá'u'lláh's teachings into a life of active service to humanity.

What Do Bahá'ís Believe About God?

> O Lord, our Lord, how majestic is your name in all the earth!   Psalms 8:1

> This is God, your Lord, and unto Him shall ye return. Is there any doubt concerning God? He hath created you and all things. The Lord of all worlds is He.[7]   The Báb

President Lincoln once told the story of "a young boy who had gone with his father on a hunting trip. While asleep on the mountainside, the boy was awakened by a meteor shower. Scared, he shook his father awake. The father said, 'Son don't be concerned about the shooting stars. Keep your eyes on the fixed stars that have long been our guides.'" In a fast-changing world, God is the only constant. He is our heavenly star, the One who is ever present and bestows His glory on all who overcome the clouds, who seek Him with their whole hearts.

God is the light and the spirit of the world. Without Him life is worthless; with Him it is peace, joy, hope, and happiness.

Thy Paradise is My love; thy heavenly home, reunion with Me. Enter therein and tarry not. This is that which hath been destined for thee in Our kingdom above and Our exalted dominion.[8]

Bahá'u'lláh

My love is My stronghold; he that entereth therein is safe and secure, and he that turneth away shall surely stray and perish.[9]   Bahá'u'lláh

How blest are those who know their need of God; the kingdom of Heaven is theirs.

Christ (Matt. 5:3)

Make My love thy treasure and cherish it even as thy very sight and life.[10]   Bahá'u'lláh

When God enters our lives, we become far more precious. Without light, a diamond is as inviting as a piece of coal. But the light brings out the diamond's brilliance and makes it special. Love of God is the light that makes us shine with hope and happiness, that brings out the best in us.

Thank God, there is God. What if we didn't have Him? Remember the small child's prayer? "O God, bless me, bless my mom, dad, and sister. But make sure you take care of yourself. If something happens to you, we're all in trouble!"

In Him all things find their highest consummation, both in this world and in the world to come.[11]   The Báb

Bahá'u'lláh refers to God as "the unknowable Essence" who stands above human thoughts. No being can ever fully know the Creator's identity or essence. The best we can do is recognize some of His names or attributes. Any image of God that we may cherish is our creation, not that of our Creator:

> Our imagination can only picture that which it
> is able to create.[12]   'Abdu'l-Bahá

Even God's supreme Messengers acknowledge their inability to know God in all His glory and grandeur. They know Him only by what He chooses to reveal to them:

> I have known Thee by Thy making known unto
> me that Thou art unknowable to anyone save
> Thyself.[13]   The Báb

Our understanding of God is very narrow, as it is confined to our own experiences. It is not much better than a child's. Here are a few questions from children's letters to God:

Dear God,
How did you know you were God?

Dear God,
Are you really invisible, or is that just a trick?

Dear God,
Are you for real? Some people don't think so. If you are, you'd better do something quick!

Dear God,
My sister never stops talking. I am getting desperate. Do you have any miracles left?

Dear God,
Thanks for all the food you have given us. I have tried most of them. Ice cream and chocolate are your best ideas.

Dear God,
Do you have to go everywhere I go?

Dear God,
They say you are smart. The people you made are weird. Can you figure them out?

Apparently, God has the same question:

> The heart is deceitful above all things...Who can understand it? I the Lord search the heart and examine the mind... Jeremiah 17:9-10

Whatever we think about God is bound by our experiences and limited to our narrow vision of reality. We can learn about the attributes of God from His Messengers, from nature, and from uncovering the mysteries within our own souls. But we can never learn the essence of God.

To awaken us to our greatness, to our spiritual destiny, and to Himself, God manifests Himself periodically through human beings known by such titles as divine Messengers, Mediators, Redeemers, Saviors, Prophets, Teachers, and Manifestations. Through them God teaches us truths beyond our reach and inspires us to purity and nobility.

Each day the sun dawns from a different point. Atmospheric changes around the earth may also alter its appearance, yet it is the same sun, always radiating with full glory. The same principle applies to God's great Messengers; they come from different places and appear to be different, yet they are one:

> The Revelation of God may be likened to the sun. No matter how innumerable its risings, there

is but one sun, and upon it depends the life of all things...

The process of the rise and setting of the Sun of Truth will thus indefinitely continue—a process that hath had no beginning and will have no end.

Well is it with him who in every Dispensation recognizeth the Purpose of God for that Dispensation, and is not deprived therefrom by turning his gaze towards the things of the past.[14]   The Báb

Because of the great favors bestowed on His Messengers, they become His most intimate and devoted disciples and friends. Since they recognize His infinite perfections, they glorify Him beyond measure. They follow His bidding and stand firm in their love and devotion to Him.

Their main goal is to teach us so that we too may learn to **know**, **love**, and **glorify** God. This knowledge, love, and devotion are the most powerful motivators in all the universe. They can uplift an individual from the depths of immorality, selfishness, despair, and gloom to the highest and richest realms of purity, peace, and perfection.

We can learn to know and love God in three ways: by looking deep into our own souls, by piercing the mysteries of the universe, and best of all, by pondering the lives and teachings of great Messengers, who give us perfectly accurate and direct knowledge about our Creator. They are the most polished and splendid Mirrors of God's glory and knowledge. Whatever they teach us is indeed God's Word.

In his book *God's Loving Words*, Dr. Ray Stedman offers this story to demonstrate the relationship between God and humanity:

> The Danish Christian philosopher Sören Kierkegaard tells the story about a king who fell in love with a peasant maiden. This king was the wealthiest, most respected, most powerful king in the entire region. No one dared oppose him or speak a word against him. But this king—as powerful and respected as he was—had a problem: How could he tell this maiden that he loved her? And how could he know for sure that she loved him?

> The very fact that he was a king—rich, famous, and powerful—was a barrier.

> He could lead an armed escort of knights to the door of her humble cottage, and he could demand, by his authority as king, that she marry him.

> But that wouldn't do. The king didn't want a fearful slave for a wife. He wanted someone who would love him, someone to share his life, someone who would be happy and eager to spend her days at his side.

> He could shower her with gifts and jewels and beautiful robes and—

> No, no, that wouldn't do either. He didn't want to buy her love. He wanted her to love him for himself, not for his gifts and his wealth.

> Somehow he had to find a way to win the maiden's love without overwhelming her, without destroying her free will. Somehow he had to make himself her equal.

So the king clothed himself in rags and went to her as a peasant. But the truly amazing thing is this: The king did not merely disguise himself as a poor man. He actually became poor! He loved this maiden so much that he renounced his throne, his wealth, and his kingly power to win her love! [15]

This beautiful parable shows how the King and Creator of the universe manifests Himself in a humble human being and subjects Himself to the requirements of nature: hunger, pain, disease, and even death. If God overwhelmed us with His infinite power and glory, we could not love Him freely. We would act more like fearful slaves.

Knowing God is the first and foremost knowledge:

> The source of all learning is the knowledge of God, exalted be His Glory, and this cannot be attained save through the knowledge of His Divine Manifestation. [16]   Bahá'u'lláh

> The purpose of God in creating man is but for him to know Him. [17]   The Báb

Knowing God does not mean simply acknowledging Him, but rather discovering His design of creation—learning how He works, how He does things, and why. Is there a test to show how much we know God? Here is one: The more we know God, the less we ask, "Why?" and the more we say, "Thanks!" Knowing God increases gratitude, and decreases grief and griping. Disappointment comes from deficiency of knowledge, from thinking that our plans for our lives are better than God's plan.

Love of God makes our hearts cheerful. Even when we feel bad, we feel good for feeling bad, for we know that the magic of His love always turns the rain into a rainbow.

It is absolutely essential to recognize that, in this world, God relates to us in two ways: by manifesting Himself and by remaining secret. Look back at your life and see how many times, at a critical point, somehow you managed, somehow "you made it." If you look at one piece or one point, you may say it was coincidence. But if you put all the points and pieces together, you realize that an unseen hand must have been at work—secretly sending you subtle signals, just strong enough to keep you from stumbling, to get you over the hurdle.

God always whispers His signals and secrets with a precise pitch—just loud enough and quiet enough—so that we can either hear them or not hear them at all:

> This is the Voice of God...the manifest and hidden Secret...[18]   Bahá'u'lláh

Only when we soften our hearts can we hear His Voice:

> Today, if you hear his voice, do not harden your hearts...   Psalms 95:7

> Incline thine ear unto the voice of thy Lord, the Lord of all mankind...[19]   Bahá'u'lláh

Only a whole-hearted desire can reveal the glory of God:

> Seek the Lord your God, you will find him if you
> look for him with all your heart and with all your
> soul.   Deuteronomy 4:29

Just as radar must be highly sensitive to a signal
while filtering out noise, so must be our souls. If
we filter out "the noise," we will hear God's voice
from every atom in the universe. Every stone,
every leaf, every bird sings His praise, except a
heart that is out of order and out of tune.

God never breaks His veil of secrecy. That would
destroy His entire design of creation. Expecting the
display of miraculous powers from God at the time
of the advent of every Redeemer is an example of
a failure to understand and appreciate this principle,
this most fundamental link between God and His
creatures.

Within the depths of every soul God has deposited
the potential to know Him:

> He hath moreover deposited within the realities
> of all created things the emblem of His recogni-
> tion, that everyone may know of a certainty that
> He is the Beginning and the End, the Manifest
> and the Hidden, the Maker and the Sustainer, the
> Omnipotent and the All-Knowing, the One Who
> heareth and perceiveth all things, He Who is
> invincible in His power and standeth supreme in
> His Own identity...[20]   The Báb

And this is another sign of knowing God: The one
who truly knows God also recognizes His Messengers. The Pharisees who rejected Jesus considered
themselves strong believers in God, yet Jesus told
them they did not know Him:

> My Father, whom you claim as your God, is the
> one who glorifies me. Though you do not know
> Him, I know Him.   Christ (John 8:54-55)

Their preoccupation with earthly power and glory
was the best evidence of their ignorance and lack
of spiritual insight. They expected God to break the
veil of secrecy and suddenly manifest His power
and majesty by giving them visible dominion and
supremacy over their enemies.

Divine Messengers provide the most direct and
obvious link between God and His creatures. By
speaking through them, God can maintain His
secrecy and still talk to us in our language, just like
another human being. It is impossible to imagine
that God could speak more directly to us than this,
short of actually revealing Himself to us as He
does to His Messengers and Redeemers.

This is an amazing phenomenon: God, the Creator
of the universe, speaking to us just like a friend
and telling us that He is our true Beloved! Yet so
many human beings refuse to accept this honor—
to be God's true lover and friend!

God respects our freedom. That is one of His
choicest gifts to us. Without it we would be like
slaves. He wants us to know Him and to love Him
by choice, not by force; by desire, not by demand.
***Every choice is both an evidence and a test of our
freedom***. The tests bring to light our hidden selves.
They show whether we are gold or mere glitters.
They allow our souls to ***choose*** and ***reveal*** a given
level of goodness and perfection. Some reach for
the sublime; others for mediocrity.

One drop out of the ocean of His bountiful grace is enough to confer upon all beings the glory of everlasting life. But inasmuch as the divine Purpose hath decreed that the true should be known from the false, and the sun from the shadow, He hath, therefore, in every season sent down upon mankind the showers of tests from His realm of glory.[21]

Bahá'u'lláh

The more we love God, the more we love one another. The closer we are to God, the closer we are to happiness. Today, many live in the darkness of unbelief. The light of God is absent in many a heart and home.

Is God present in the houses of worship? "A Sunday school teacher asked her students to write a letter to God. One little girl wrote, 'Dear God, we had a great time at church today. I wish you could have been there.'"

Seeing and recognizing God and His Messengers requires spiritual sight. As much of God is visible as we have eyes to see.

To know, to love, and to glorify God is the noblest and most supreme honor. Every human being is invited to partake of this honor, to celebrate His praise with the utmost joy and ecstasy:

Bestir thyself, and magnify, before the entire creation, the name of God, and celebrate His praise, in such wise that all created things may be regenerated and made new. Speak, and hold not thy peace.[22]　　Bahá'u'lláh

For every one of you his paramount duty is to choose for himself that on which no other may infringe and none usurp from him. Such a thing... is the love of God, could ye but perceive it.[23]

Bahá'u'lláh

We were not made to eat, to sleep, and to exercise. We were not made to work, to wash, and to watch TV. We were not made to make money, to build beautiful houses, and to buy the finest furniture and jewelry. We were not even made to get married and live happily ever after. We were made for one reason and one purpose:

- To learn as much as we can about God,

- To learn to love Him passionately, perfectly, and unconditionally, and

- To glorify Him and thank Him for making all these possible, for creating and loving us, for giving us the chance to be His lovers and His most sublime creation, and for all the infinite gifts, pleasures, and bounties He has provided for us.

If we spend our lives for any purpose other than knowing Him, if we live for any reason other than loving Him and glorifying Him, it is like going into a theater that presents the most majestic and beautiful movie and, instead of enjoying the splendid scenes, hearing the heavenly music, and basking in the company of friends and loved ones, we sit down, close our eyes, and go to sleep! What a sense of loss and failure, what a sense of anger, grief, and remorse, when we wake up to discover that the movie has ended, that the opportunity is gone forever!

The Relationship Between God, His Mediators, and Humankind

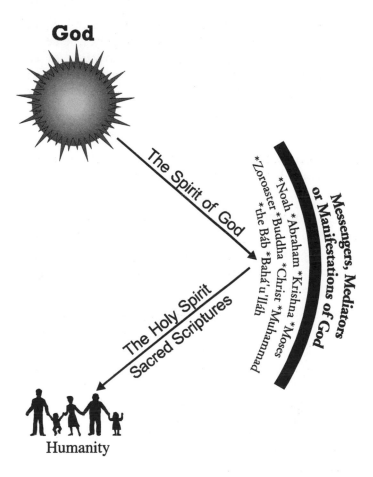

Be ye assured, that the works and acts of each and every one of these Manifestations of God, nay whatever pertaineth unto them, and whatsoever they may manifest in the future, are all ordained by God, and are a reflection of His Will and Purpose.[24]
Bahá'u'lláh

From Him proceed their knowledge and power; from Him is derived their sovereignty. The beauty of their countenance is but a reflection of His image, and their revelation a sign of His deathless glory.[25]
Bahá'u'lláh

The Lord God of your fathers...hath sent me...
Moses (Exodus 3:15)

I do nothing on my own authority, but in all that I say, I have been taught by my Father.
Christ (John 8:28)

Only what is revealed to me do I follow.
Muhammad (Qur'án 6:50)

Not of Mine own volition have I revealed Myself, but God, of His own choosing, hath manifested Me.[26]
Bahá'u'lláh

The sweetest and most sublime music comes from the beating of a heart in tune with the knowledge and love of God. Our attachment to God gives us the strength to cope with the stress and distress of living. It protects the flame and fuels the candle. "A lady went to her doctor and said, 'Doctor, I know I've been working too hard, but I don't want you to tell me to stop burning the candle at both ends. What I need is more wax.'" Love of God is an everlasting flame.

One God
Many Messengers

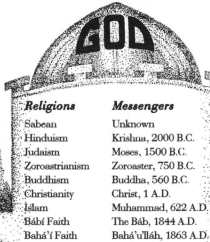

Religions	Messengers
Sabean	Unknown
Hinduism	Krishna, 2000 B.C.
Judaism	Moses, 1500 B.C.
Zoroastrianism	Zoroaster, 750 B.C.
Buddhism	Buddha, 560 B.C.
Christianity	Christ, 1 A.D.
Islam	Muhammad, 622 A.D.
Bábí Faith	The Báb, 1844 A.D.
Bahá'í Faith	Bahá'u'lláh, 1863 A.D.

I shall come again and receive you to myself.   Christ

I am the Alpha and the Omega, the First and the Last, the Beginning and the End.   Christ

Whenever there is decay of righteousness...then I Myself come forth...for the sake of firmly establishing righteousness. I am born from age to age.   Krishna

I am not the first Buddha who came upon the earth, nor shall I be the last. In due time another Buddha will arise...He shall reveal to you the same eternal truths which I have taught you.   Buddha

All these holy, divine Manifestations are one. They have served one God, promulgated the same truth...and reflected the same light...In name and form they differ, but in reality They agree and are the same.   Bahá'u'lláh

The Revelation of God may be likened to the sun. No matter how innumerable its risings, there is but one sun, and upon it depends the life of all things.   The Báb

> The Lord's unfailing love surrounds the man who trusts in him. Rejoice in the Lord and be glad, you righteous; sing, all you who are upright in heart!
> Psalms 32:10-11

> With thee is the fountain of life. In thy light shall we see light.
> Psalms 36:9

> In thy presence is fullness of joy; at thy right hand are pleasures for evermore.
> Psalms 16:11

No joy can compare with the joy of knowing, loving, serving, and glorifying God. The purpose of religion is to spread and strengthen this knowledge, love and devotion, and to bring them into every heart and every home. Without God, the world is a place of gloom and darkness, and the heart an abode of despair and emptiness.

Like an old tree that begins to rot and break down, when a religion loses its spiritual and transforming powers, it becomes an instrument of division and discord rather than of unity, harmony, and love. It promotes rote learning and superstition rather than reasoning and understanding; consequently, believers begin to lose their faith and their sense of connection with other human beings. They wonder why God does not care anymore, they blame Him for their troubles and sufferings, and eventually they ignore His counsels. When people lose touch with God, they also lose touch with themselves. Knowledge of God leads to knowledge of self; ignorance of God leads to ignorance of self.

Love of God turns us from mortal to immortal beings. It changes the monotony of daily chores into an ever-advancing journey of hope and fulfillment, of wonder, exhilaration, and ecstasy. Today many are deprived of this most exciting dimension of human life; they see the mud holes, but miss the rainbow.

The Bahá'í Faith has proved capable of restoring God's love to the heart of humanity by making religion rational and relevant to our time. Bahá'ís believe that Bahá'u'lláh's Revelation is a clear proof that God *cares* and *always will*. In the teachings of the Bahá'í Faith, we can find peace, hope, and harmony. By the guidance it provides we can resolve the world's distressing problems. Through Bahá'u'lláh's teachings we can build a heavenly kingdom, a glorious civilization that has been the promise of all the great Messengers and the hope of humanity since the dawn of history.

Why Do We Need a New Faith?

Deep in our souls we know that there is more to life than running the rat race, that there must be another race: for spiritual advancement, for an enduring hope and purpose. Deep in our souls we also know that while on earth we have a special mission, that we matter more than we think, and that we must accomplish something that will outlive our lives.

We all have dreams...We all want to believe deep down in our souls that we have a special gift, that we can make a difference, that we can touch others in a special way, and that we can make the world a better place. At one time in our lives, we all had a vision for the quality of life that we desire and deserve. Yet, for many of us, those dreams have become so shrouded in the frustrations and routines of daily life that we no longer even make an effort to accomplish them. For far too many, the dream has dissipated—and with it, so has the will to shape our destinies. Many have lost that sense of certainty that creates the winner's edge.[27]

That dreaming and dormant longing in the soul can come to life only by the light of the knowledge of God, as reflected in His latest Mirror or Messenger. That knowledge transforms the soul just as a fire transforms wax into light. When the knowledge is allowed to reach the soul, the light shines and despair vanishes. Today, we see a lot of wax but little light in the heart of humanity. The evidences of despair and darkness are all around us.

The family is the basis of society. Like dominoes, when the family falls, everything falls. Today, the family is in grave danger. A teenager told his mother, "I am tired of living in this house. I want to go where there is love, peace, joy, and excitement." His mother rose and started walking towards him. The teenager yelled, "Don't try to stop me! I have made up my mind!" His mother said, "Stop you? I want to join you!"

William Bennett, former U.S. Secretary of Education, issued a report on "the index of leading cultural indicators,"[28] in which he compared some vital statistics about family life in America. He found that during the last 30 years:

- Divorces increased 400 percent.
- Out-of-wedlock births increased 400 percent.
- The number of children living in single-parent homes increased 300 percent.
- Reports of child abuse increased 340 percent...[29]

In the United States, domestic violence is the leading cause of injury to married couples aged 15 to 45, more than all injuries caused by muggings and car accidents combined. President Clinton cited this fact, and added that in recent years domestic violence has increased three times faster than crime. In a U.N. conference on social development, it was announced that 30 percent of girls throughout the world are sexually abused, and once they are married, 50 percent are abused by their husbands.

A comedian once said, "Keep your houses unlocked, so that in times of danger you can escape quickly." The comedian may have a point; statistics indicate that one's home is the most dangerous place. More people are killed, beaten, and abused in their home than anywhere else!

The suicide rate is perhaps the best concrete index of the psychological and spiritual health of a nation. Suicide has increased in most nations, especially among young people. In the last thirty years, the percentage of young Americans who attempt suicide has increased 500 percent.[30] In many other countries such as Canada, Finland, France, Israel, the Netherlands, New Zealand, Spain, Switzerland, and Thailand, suicide rates among young people have also increased dramatically.[31]

A recent "Who's Who?" survey of 2,000 outstanding students in America showed that 30 percent of them had considered attempting suicide. These are individuals at the prime of their lives, when they should be the happiest. "In the summer of 1990, a special commission issued a report on the health of today's adolescent. This team of prominent experts wrote, 'Never before has one generation of American teenagers been less healthy, less cared for or less prepared for life.'"[32] In still another study, "More than half of young Americans between the ages 16 and 24 said they had thought about killing themselves."[33]

A Christian association recently studied the attitudes of nearly 4,000 young people aged 11-18. Of every one hundred of these youths, 80 attended an evangelical church weekly, and 86 said they had made a commitment to trust Christ as their Savior and Lord.[34] Here are some of their findings:

- 66 percent of those surveyed said they had lied to their parents or another adult in the last three months. Almost that many (59 percent) had lied to their peers.

- 55 percent said they were confused.

- 50 percent said they were suffering from stress.

- 46 percent said they were always tired.

- Many others said they were cheating, smoking, gambling, watching X-rated movies and engaging in premarital sex.[35]

The researchers ask, "What is happening to our kids? Why aren't they adopting our values? And what can we do about it?"[36] Confidence in organized religion has been falling. In 1993:

> The PPRC Index, a figure that provides an overall assessment of the state of American religion, was 649, the lowest ever...The index reflects belief in God, church membership/attendance and confidence in the clergy, the church and religion itself.[37]

Sexual abuse of children is the most evident and alarming sign of spiritual starvation. What are the statistics?

- One out of every four American women is sexually abused before she reaches 18.
- Girls are twice more likely to be sexually abused than boys.
- Family members—fathers, stepfathers, uncles, grandfathers, and brothers—are the most frequent abusers of children under age 11.[38]

The statistics on mental illness, depression, alcoholism, drug addiction, violence, and crime are equally alarming. Our youths are the most vulnerable. One third of all crime is committed by children and youths 10 to 17 years old. Among the top killers of our youths are homicide, suicide, and AIDS.

According to a highly respected textbook in abnormal psychology, about one fifth of the American population suffers from mental disorders or drug addiction.[39]

Consider the increase in crime in England and Wales per 100,000 population:

1955	1,000
1961	1,750
1971	3,400
1981	5,600
1991	10,000 — ten times the rate of 1955 and forty times that of 1901.[40]

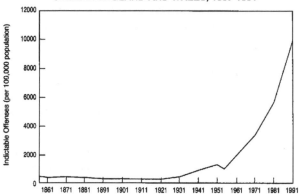

CRIME IN ENGLAND AND WALES, 1857-1991

Source: For 1857-1980: B.R. Mitchell, *British Historical Statistics* (Cambridge, England, 1988), pp. 776-778; for 1981-1991: Home Office *Criminal Statistics*.[41]

What caused the decline of the Roman Empire? About two centuries ago, Edward Gibbon, the author of the classic *The Rise and Fall of the Roman Empire*, listed these reasons, which look disturbingly familiar:

- Loss of dignity and sanctity of the home, and an increased divorce rate

- Higher taxes and spending of public moneys

- A craze for pleasure and brutal sports

- The building of gigantic armaments when the real enemy was within
- The decay of religion and the impotence of religious leaders[42]

As historians tell us, if we fail to learn the lessons of history, we will have to repeat them. What happens to a woman who forgets her past? She becomes a child. What happens to a child who fails to benefit from his experience? His body grows, but not his mind. The same happens to nations and the world. The mid-19th Century marked a turning point in human history. The spiritual state of the world had declined so much that it required revival. The following statement by Abraham Lincoln during the Civil War shows the world trends up to his time:

> We have been preserved these many years in peace and prosperity...we have grown in wealth and power as no other nation has ever grown. But we have forgotten God. We have forgotten the gracious hand which preserved us in peace... and we have vainly imagined that all these blessings were produced by some superior wisdom and virtue of our own. Intoxicated with unbroken success, we have become too self-sufficient to feel the necessity of redeeming and preserving grace. Too proud to pray to the God who made us.[43]

Today people have forgotten who they are and how great they are. A young man named John went to a big city. The sight of crowds frightened him. He said to himself, "What if I went to sleep, woke up, but could not find myself in the crowd!" He talked to a man named Joe about his fears. Joe told him to put a tag with his name around his ankle. John liked the idea and followed it. When he went to sleep, Joe took the tag from John's ankle and put it on his own. When John woke up, he saw the tag and thought Joe was him. Seized with fear, he exclaimed, "Joe, if you are me, then, for heaven's sake, who and where am I?"

Not only have people forgotten who they are, they have also lost track of where they are going. A driver got lost on a country road. He stopped and asked a little girl, "Do you know which way is south?" "No!" "Do you know Highway 20?" "No!" "Do you know a gas station around here?" "No!" In desperation, the driver asked, "Do you know anything?" The little girl said, "I know one thing. I ain't lost!"

Faith gives meaning and purpose to everything we do and is the only thing that remains when everything else is gone. "Once when a precocious six-year-old displayed her aversion to a proper diet, her father exasperatedly asked, 'Child, you don't care for vegetables, salad, fruits, or fish—what do you like?' Turning her wide brown eyes on him, she demurely answered, 'Why, I like you, Daddy!'"

Noted historian Arnold Toynbee stated, "Of the twenty-two civilizations that appear in history, nineteen of them collapsed when they reached the moral state the United States is in now."[44] Eminent historian Will Durant indicated there is no example in history to show that we can have morality without religion. We find many political leaders in former communist countries who were trained to be atheists and yet today they acknowledge the human need for spirituality. According to Vladimir Shlapntokh, who has conducted public opinion polls for *Pravda*:

> Soviet leaders are looking for help in the form of the restoration of old religious norms...compassion, grace, forgiveness, charity, and other virtues previously presented as elements of bourgeois decadence. Leaders [see] religion as a means of halting Soviet society's accelerating demoralization.[45]

As Jesus said, "Man cannot live by bread alone" (Matthew 4:4). The Word of God is the heavenly food that satisfies the spirit. A beggar asked a woman for money. She offered to buy him lunch. He said, "I've had three lunches while trying to get a dime!" He could not live by food alone.

Spirituality is the yeast that elevates our attitude. Without it, we remain stagnant, like a heavy lump of dough. Adler, the noted psychologist, tells about "a group of people who were crowded together, trying to sleep on the floor of a great auditorium during the war, but one woman kept them awake with her pitiful cries, 'Oh, God, I'm so thirsty!' Finally, someone got up in the dark and brought her a glass of water. They could hear the woman gurgle the water down, but suddenly, they heard her again moaning, 'Oh God, how thirsty I was!'"

According to a CNN report, some experts believe that if people paid their taxes honestly, the yearly deficit in the U. S. budget would be wiped out. The IRS is the most feared agency in the United States, yet that strong fear does not overcome greed. Only inner auditing before God can prevent people from cheating.

Most of the problems we face in the world are caused by a loss of identity, a lack of purpose, and a loss of faith. Historically, when human life has descended to a critical point, God has sent a new Teacher or Messenger to lift our spirits and enrich our lives. We have already passed that low point.

Chuck Colson, an eloquent and enlightened writer and spokesman for Christianity, gave the following message on a Christian radio station:

> Pollster George Gallup compared the ethical behavior of Americans who attend church regularly and those who never attend. He compiled candid admissions from people who call in sick when they are not, who puff their resumes, who cheat on income taxes. Astonishingly, Gallup reported "little difference in the ethical views and behavior of the churched and the unchurched."
>
> In a similar vein, religion reporter Terry Mattingly recently cited surveys showing that students at Christian colleges cheat on exams at the same rates as students at secular colleges.
>
> What does all this tell us? That many Christians are guilty of compartmentalizing our lives into separate boxes so that our faith never influences our every-day attitudes and opinions. Many of us are as fragmented in our minds as any double agent.[46]

In his book *The Body*, Mr. Colson wrote:

The roots of the church's identity crisis are found in the consumer mentality so pervasive in our culture...People flit about in search of what suits their taste at the moment. It's what some have called the 'McChurch' mentality...Thus, the church becomes just another retail outlet, faith just another commodity.[47]

Today, religion has lost its grip on the spiritual life of the world. "A minister glared down at Sam and roared, 'And are you, my son, a soldier in the army of the Lord?' Surprised at being singled out, Sam replied anxiously, 'Y-yes sir, I am.' 'Then why,' pressed the minister, 'do we see you here only at Christmas?' Thinking quickly, Sam replied, 'Would you believe, sir, I'm in the secret service?'" In this age, many of the faithful have gone from active service to secret service.

Today, religion has been turned into a talk show. "Adlai Stevenson told the story of a backsliding man who was so inspired by an eloquent preacher that he leaped out of his seat and yelled, 'Lord God, take me and use me—in an advisory capacity.'" The talking and avoiding must be changed into doing:

> The essence of faith is fewness of words and abundance of deeds; he whose words exceed his deeds, know verily his death is better than his life.[48]   Bahá'u'lláh

"A rabbi and a soap maker went for a walk together. The soap maker said, 'What good is religion? Look at all the trouble and misery of the world, after thousands of years of teaching about goodness and truth and peace. If religion is good and true, why should this be?' The rabbi said nothing. They continued walking until he noticed a child playing in the gutter. Then the rabbi said, 'Look at that child. You make soap and say that it makes people clean, but see the dirt on that youngster. Of what good is soap? With all the soap in the world, over all these years, that child is still filthy. I wonder how effective soap is, after all!' The soap maker protested. 'But, Rabbi, soap cannot do any good unless it is used!' 'Exactly,' replied the Rabbi. 'Exactly!'"

What is the most significant source of moral values? Religion. How can moral values be strengthened? By making religion rational and relevant. Suppose you have a suit. You either gain or lose weight, or you simply grow up. What happens to the suit? It loses its suitability. The same thing happens to old ideas and institutions. Bahá'u'lláh makes religion suitable to our time and to our needs and increased capacity.

To survive and prosper, we must acquire these assets and virtues:

- a sense of dignity and nobility
- a cosmic and global perspective; a feeling of being connected to all the universe and all humanity
- knowledge of an undying and eternal purpose; a new vision about who we are, what on earth we are doing, and where we are going
- a rational understanding of religion
- a new renaissance of morality and a strong commitment to ethical values

- an intimate relationship with God, who is the source of our noblest hope and our most profound and enduring happiness

Without the new vision and new perspective, we operate on a level of narrow self-interest and confusion. Hedonism becomes our hope, and pleasure our prime purpose in life.

"William Barker tells about a machinist with the Ford motor company in Detroit who had, over a period of years, 'borrowed' various tools from the company but never bothered to return them. While this practice was not condoned, it was more or less accepted by management, and nothing was done about it. The machinist, however, experienced a religious conversion. He was baptized and became a devout believer. Even more importantly, he took his baptism seriously. The very next morning he arrived at work loaded down with tools he had taken from the company during the years. The foreman was so astonished and impressed by his action, that he cabled Mr. Ford, who was visiting a European plant, and explained the entire story in detail. Immediately Mr. Ford cabled back: 'Dam up the Detroit River, and baptize the entire city!'" Not only the residents of Detroit but all the citizens of the planet need a "baptism of the spirit."

Like everything else that comes in touch with human beings, religion gradually becomes polluted with hypocrisy, fanaticism, dogmatism, prejudice, irrationality, emotionalism, divisiveness, worldliness, complacency, and pride. When the pollution reaches a critical point, God in His Wisdom sends a new

Redeemer or Messenger with a new outpouring of knowledge, love, and wisdom. But by then people have become fully addicted to the age-old pollutants. They draw comfort from their prejudices, superstitions, and illusions. Abandoning them causes withdrawal symptoms. Sometimes, some of the addicted recognize the danger of being exposed to the pollutants and try to install a few filters. But the pollutants are so strong, and the state of sickness so severe, that filters make no difference.

True faith elevates the human spirit to peace and ecstasy, it inspires an unshakable hope and happiness. It is a heavenly wine that intoxicates the soul. Today its powers are diluted, its influence diminished. It is in desperate need of reviving. "A young man announced during the children's sermon, 'I'm against liquor-by-the drink.' 'That's good,' said his pastor. 'But why are you against it?' 'I'm against it because my mother's against it,' the boy said. The pastor should have stopped while he was ahead, but he didn't 'Why is your mother against it?' 'She's against it,' the young man said 'because she says they water those drinks down too much.'"

Picture God as the most beautiful and majestic star veiled behind the clouds. In each age or dispensation, He removes a bit of the veil and allows His glory to become more visible. Without looking up, basking in His beauty, and rejoicing in the knowledge of His presence, we are doomed to a life of quiet desperation. Without the light of His love, we can live only in the twilight of doubt, fear, and spiritual apathy:

True knowledge, therefore, is the knowledge of God, and this is none other than the recognition of His Manifestation in each Dispensation.[49]

The Báb

Today, many search for their god in gold and for their well-being in wine and wealth. Many think the true remedy is to raise their standard of living. They set standards for poverty, so that the poor can be identified and uplifted. What we need to raise first is the *spiritual* standard of living. Spiritual poverty and starvation are threatening our very survival. The following are among the harshest words addressed to the people of our time, especially to those who seek their god in gold and search in vain for their well-being in wealth:

> You say, "I am rich; I have acquired wealth and do not need a thing." But you do not realize that you are wretched, pitiful, poor, blind, and naked. I counsel you to buy from me gold refined in the fire, so you can become rich; and white clothes to wear, so you can cover your shameful nakedness; and salve to put on your eyes, so you can see.   Christ (Rev. 3:17-18)

Left to ourselves, we are mere rocks and pebbles. Only by loving God and living by His laws can we turn the rocks into rubies and the pebbles into pearls.

> No created thing shall ever attain its paradise unless it appeareth in its highest prescribed degree of perfection. For instance, this crystal representeth the paradise of the stone whereof its substance is composed. Likewise there are various stages in

the paradise for the crystal itself...So long as it was stone it was worthless, but if it attaineth the excellence of ruby—a potentiality which is latent in it—how much a carat will it be worth? Consider likewise every created thing.

Man's highest station, however, is attained through faith in God in every Dispensation and by acceptance of what hath been revealed by Him...[50]   The Báb

All the facts presented lead us to this conclusion: There is an overwhelming need for the renewal of religion, for a faith that can transform our lives, that can lift us from worldliness and apathy to spirituality and ecstasy.

Is There Any Evidence That the Bahá'í Faith Transforms Lives?

If a religion does not transform lives, it is worthless. The purpose of food is to provide nourishment. If it doesn't, it is not food. The purpose of faith is to bring us peace of mind, hope, love, purpose, joy, and contentment. If it doesn't, it is not faith but fantasy.

Many years ago, I conducted a study of a group of college students who had become Bahá'ís. The study pointed to immediate and often dramatic changes in virtually every aspect of their lives: personal, social, spiritual, and academic. An unexpected finding was that their overall grade point averages rose substantially. Their new-found faith increased their sense of well-being and motivation. It gave them more energy to study.

Instead of showing the transforming power of the Bahá'í Faith on other people's lives, let me give you just a glimpse of its influence on my own life. This information may give you a better understanding of why I wrote this book, why I wanted to share Bahá'u'lláh's message with others. It is for that reason alone that I will say something about myself.

The difference the Bahá'í Faith has made in my life is the difference between living in gloom and living in gladness, between living in apathy and living in ecstasy. To be brief, I will focus on how my faith affects my work. As an instructor I tell my students that what they need before anything else is a positive attitude: looking for the best in themselves and others and having hope for the future. I teach them that we are what we think. In the absence of positive thinking, our days turn into gloomy and scary nights. In its presence, the gloom and fear turn into gladness and hope, into ecstasy and adventure. A positive attitude gives us the strength and the desire to live and give life to others.

We always have a choice to see either good or bad or both in every experience, in everything that happens. "The squeaky tenor had just concluded. The applause was less than warm. But one member of the audience was exclaiming, 'Extraordinary! Wonderful! Unbelievable!'

'Pardon me,' said a puzzled man sitting in the next seat. 'You astound me. I think I may claim some knowledge of the subject, and I think his voice was very poor.'

'Voice?' said the other man. 'I wasn't thinking of his voice. I was praising his nerve!'"

Of course, the best way to teach is by example. I treat my students as special gifts, with a love and respect they have seldom experienced. While many professors complain about unmotivated and ungrateful students, I bask in a constant stream of appreciation and gratitude. Many of my students are astonished by my positive attitude. They can't understand how anyone in this gloomy world can be so highly motivated and positive. They don't learn the secret until the last day in the semester. On that day, they learn about the positive forces that have shaped my life: mainly my faith and my mother, who also gained her enthusiasm and zest for life from the Bahá'í Faith.

As a rule, I find a few negative students at the beginning of every semester, and I make an effort to win their hearts by making them feel special. I compliment them, smile at them, and speak with them after class. These favors, along with the overwhelming positive force generated in class, eradicate or at least subdue their negativism. After years of seeing significant transformations in thousands of my students, I am still astonished by the power of unconditional love and a positive attitude.

Let me cite an example of helping a negative person become more positive. I have been using a handout that has been quite popular. Recently an extremely negative student found fault with one point in that handout. She stated her view with strong emotions as if to invite a fight. In response, I laughed and said, "You are so creative! I have been using this handout for ten years and have never heard anything negative about it. You are the first one to find a fault! Thank you for being so creative!" She was utterly surprised—and disappointed—and had no other weapon ready to fire. That response, and a steady stream of positive energy generated by other students, transformed her attitude. On the last day of the semester she embraced and kissed a student she had offended earlier. This resulted in a warm and cheerful ovation from everyone in class.

I try to practice the principle of oneness, perhaps the foremost teaching of Bahá'u'lláh, in every facet of my life. Early in the semester I tell my students, "We are the cells of one body. We are one. Your problem is my problem. When something bothers you, please talk to me. I consider helping you and serving you a privilege and an honor. Do not hesitate to come." As an example, this semester I worked with a young student whose high school sweetheart, whom he loved dearly, was killed in an accident. It took several months before the deep gloom and sadness on his face turned into a smile.

To extend my positive influence, every week I wear a special button that speaks for peace, love, and unity, and against prejudice, ignorance, and spiritual poverty.

We should note that only God transforms lives. All we can do is connect to Him and turn His power into light. Without Him, we are helpless.

I could cite hundreds of examples of transformation, some dramatic, to show Bahá'u'lláh's incredible power in changing lives. But that is beyond the scope of this book. Transforming lives, changing the negative into positive, eradicating long-cherished prejudices and illusions is not easy. When transformation occurs on a large scale, as it does among those who become Bahá'ís, it is evidence that God's hand is at work. That is why Christ said, "God's wisdom is proved by its result" (Matt. 11:19), and "Ye shall know them by their fruits" (Matt. 7:16). Buddha declared the same message—"This is the true law of life: from good must come good, and from evil must come evil."

Climbing to the mountaintop requires effort. Only divine power can take us to the top. 'Abdu'l-Bahá tells a story about a pious man who invited a drunkard to follow him and pray with him for 40 nights to see how his life would be transformed. The drunkard smiled and said, "Come with me for only one minute and see how *your* life will be transformed!"[51]

If you read this book with an open mind and a humble heart, you will experience a major transformation in your life. You will say, "I didn't know I was missing so much!"

We are all prisoners of our surroundings, of family and culturally imposed limitations. True knowledge, like a beam of light, leads us beyond the prison. Once we see the beautiful scenery outside, our vision expands and a return to the prison becomes impossible. Taking that first step is all we need to do, yet many are unwilling to do even that much. Reading a book about the Bahá'í Faith is an example of stepping beyond the barriers of family and culturally imposed limitations.

What Are the Two Most Critical Questions Every Seeker of Truth Should Ask?

God gave us the gift of reason to *find* the truth and the energizing force of feelings to *fall in love* with the truth. Both must be used. We can neither find the truth with feelings nor fall in love with the truth by reason alone.

Among the most serious distortions in religion is the use of emotions, personal needs, and desires in place of proof and evidence. When it comes to religion, many act as rationally as a 3-year-old girl named Jan who visited her grandparents. Later three other children joined her. There were altogether four children and twelve cookies. The hostess said, "There are only three cookies for each of you. Please take no more." But Jan took four and started eating one of them. "You can't do that!" said the hostess. "Please put the fourth one back." "I can't!" exclaimed Jan. "I ate the fourth one first."

Since we have been exposed to religious sects whose prime mission is to impose beliefs with no regard for reason, we have been forced to build defenses to protect our souls against zealous intruders. We have become skeptical of all groups without making any distinctions. A person who is robbed, or whose house has been broken into, avoids and builds walls against all strangers, even perhaps suspecting honored guests. This is unfortunate, for suspicion has caused avoidance and an epidemic of intellectual and spiritual apathy and indifference. To restore people's confidence and love for truth and knowledge, we need to infuse religion with reason. Reason never fears the truth. It is always emotions that escape or build protective shields against the truth.

In recognizing or testing the truth of a religion, we should begin with two questions:

- Why have the overwhelming majority of people always rejected God's Messengers?

- What makes *my* religion true?

By clarifying or resolving these two questions, *we open new doors that will lead us to an objective knowledge of truth*. When we realize that most of those who met Noah, Abraham, Moses, or Jesus failed to recognize their greatness, we become more humble. A mountain climber who knows that many others have tried and failed to conquer the crest of a mountain will not be complacent about victory. He or she will examine every evidence, will follow every lead, will investigate every clue that might explain why other climbers could not make it, and how he or she might overcome the obstacles.

Similarly, when we examine the reasons why we believe in our own religion, or what makes our religion true for us, we descend from the hazy realm of mystery, supposition, and assumption to the firm facts of reality. We learn to become more objective in judging our beliefs. Our lives are so rushed, we seldom stop to think and meditate. A moment of pondering is worth more than a thousand years of wandering.

Bahá'u'lláh often asks the followers of all religions to compare the proofs they have for their own faith with those He presents for His Faith:

> Repeat the gaze, O people, and consider the testimony of God and His proof which are in your possession, and compare them unto the Revelation sent down unto you in this Day, that the truth, the infallible truth, may be indubitably manifested unto you.[52]

If you follow a given religion, take a few minutes and respond to these questions:

- Have you ever seriously contemplated or investigated the reasons for which you believe in your own faith? If not, why?

- If you have, what reasons did you find?

- How would you respond if someone asked you, "Why do you believe in your own faith?"

- If you do not believe in any religion, list the proofs that would convince you that a person speaks not his own word, but the Word of God.

Please do respond in writing to the preceding four questions. For this book to be of real value, you need to participate. The purpose of writing is to make you as objective as possible. Few people look for reasons behind their beliefs. Any effort that will diminish emotional and subjective responses and increase thoughtful objectivity is worthwhile.

To enhance your motivation, ask yourself these questions:

- Is it wise to go through my life without knowing why I have adopted my beliefs?

- Choosing a spiritual path is the most important decision in my life. Should I not give it my most serious thoughts?

- When I choose a spouse, a career, or a college, I investigate to find the best choice. Even when I buy a house, a car, or a suit, I spend time and effort to find the best. Is my religion less significant than a house, a car, or a suit?

- I may never have thought about these questions, but should I continue to ignore them all my life?

- If I do not think about them now, when will I?

The blank space after each of the four questions is provided to show you the enormous significance of this project. If you do not like to write in the book, use a separate sheet of paper and attach it to the page. You will gain enormous benefits from responding to these seemingly simple but supremely significant questions. Now go back to the questions and write your responses, if you have not done so already.

Why Have People Always Denied God's Messengers?

You always resist the Holy Spirit! Was there ever a prophet your fathers did not persecute? They even killed those who predicted the coming of the Righteous One.   Acts 7:51-52

The Revelation which, from time immemorial, hath been acclaimed as the Purpose and Promise of all the Prophets of God, and the most cherished Desire of His Messengers, hath now, by virtue of the pervasive Will of the Almighty and at His irresistible bidding, been revealed unto men. The advent of such a Revelation hath been heralded in all the sacred Scriptures. Behold how, notwithstanding such an announcement, mankind hath strayed from its path and shut out itself from its glory.[53]   Bahá'u'lláh

Knowing the answer to this question—Why do people always deny their Messengers?—is absolutely essential for every seeker of truth. It helps us understand human nature. It reveals how people like us have behaved in similar circumstances in the past. It helps us to draw from the collective experience and wisdom of many generations.

Thinking about this question makes us humble. It helps us descend from the inflated and floating clouds of our dreams, illusions, assumptions, and fantasies to the cold facts of reality. Studying this question is like doing research to learn the secrets of success and failure. It is like finding out why millions died in an earthquake, while other millions managed to survive. It is like discovering why millions succeed at school, while other millions fail; why some companies prosper, while others go bankrupt; why some individuals live healthy and long lives, while others die early; why some parents raise well-adjusted and spiritual children, and why others fail. In all these cases we would be eager to know the reasons behind people's success and failure. Should we make an exception about religion? No, we should be even more eager, more concerned, because the consequences of our choices are everlasting. Bahá'u'lláh invites us repeatedly to avoid fantasy thinking and to engage in factual thinking:

Consider the past. How many, both high and low, have, at all times, yearningly awaited the advent of the Manifestations of God...How often have they expected His coming, how frequently have they prayed that...the promised Beauty...be made manifest to all the world. And whensoever...the light of the Unseen did shine above the horizon of the celestial might, they all denied Him, and turned away from His face—the face of God Himself. Refer ye, to verify this truth, to that which hath been recorded in every sacred Book.

Ponder for a moment, and reflect upon that which hath been the cause of such denial on the part of those who have searched with such earnestness and longing. Their attack hath been more fierce than tongue or pen can describe.[54]

Now take a few minutes to respond to the second most vital question every truth seeker must ask. List here the reasons you believe God's great Messengers and Redeemers have always been rejected:

1.

2.

3.

4.

5.

Now compare your list with this list:

- Being apathetic, having no interest in religion.

- Following the majority, assuming they are the best judges.

- Depending on religious leaders who regard tradition as equivalent to spiritual truth.

- Feeling satisfied and complacent in one's comfort zone.

- Fearing the loss of one's beliefs.

- Failing to understand the symbolism behind prophecies.

- Expecting earth-shaking or miraculous events. (Christ was expected to be a powerful king.)

- Being too busy; not finding time to devote to spiritual matters.

- Being worldly and selfish; not looking beyond self-interest.

- Not wanting to alienate friends or family members.

- Fearing a loss of status.

- Being emotionally attached to one's beliefs or traditions.

- Lacking knowledge; not hearing the new message.

Most, perhaps all, of these reasons can be summarized in these words: ***unawareness*** and ***closed-mindedness***. Those to whom God's Messengers were sent either did not look or, if they ***did*** look, saw ***only*** what they ***wanted*** to see. The next story shows the power of feelings in human judgment.

"A little girl had misbehaved and her mother told her to go to the corner, and said very harshly, 'You will sit there until your father gets home.' The little girl stuck out her lip and said, 'I'll stand in the corner, but I won't sit in the corner.' Her mother took her shoulders and forcibly sat her down. When the father came home, he asked the little girl what she was doing sitting in the corner. She said defiantly, 'My head tells me I'm sitting in the corner, but my heart tells me I'm still standing.'" This is how most people relate to religion. Their hearts rule their heads.

The way God's Messengers have been treated is the best evidence of the power of feelings in human life. Suppose you expect your greatest and most honored guest. You are so proud of receiving him, you decorate your house with the most beautiful flowers, buy expensive furniture, and prepare the most delicious foods. But when your honored guest arrives, you curse him, kick him, and kill him! How strange! How bewildering! How incredible! This is how Jesus and all the other great Messengers were treated. People did to them what they would do to their worst enemies. This is not something that happened only in ancient times, centuries ago. It also happened in the 19th Century.

If people have always rejected their Messengers, what makes us believe that this time it will be any different? Have the people of our time suddenly turned into saints and angels? "The way of the world is to praise dead saints and persecute living ones." "History teaches us that man learns nothing from history."

Do Miracles Prove the Station of God's Messengers?

When asked, "Why do you believe in your religion?" most people think first of miracles. For instance, Muslims attribute astonishing miracles to Muhammad. And they have testimonials (traditions) to support their claim. When confronted with the same question, many Christians think of the birth and resurrection of Jesus. They believe these were His ultimate proofs. More liberal Christians think of Jesus Himself: His words and deeds. Of course, many base their faith on both Jesus as a person and His miracles. Those who consider miracles the prime proofs become disappointed when they learn that many "pagans" also try to prove their beliefs by miracles. For the "pagans" present glowing testimonials about their gods; they attribute to them the most astonishing wonders. How can we tell who is right, who is wrong? We face an impasse, an impossible task. Miracles are definitely unreliable, especially for those who have not witnessed them.

Jesus performed many miracles, but He repeatedly asked people to keep them secret.

> See that no one knows about this.
> Christ (Matt. 9:30)

> See that you don't tell anyone.   Christ (Matt. 8:4)

People were so fascinated by Jesus' miracles, they disobeyed His instructions. "But they went out and spread the news [of miracles] about him all over that region" (Matt. 9:31). We can discern a sense of desperation in this question by Jesus:

> Will none of you ever believe without seeing signs and portents?
> John 4:48

Would God use as evidence of His power and presence something that He condemns?

> Why do you quarrel with Me? Why do you put the Lord to the test?
> Exodus 17:2

> A wicked and adulterous [disloyal] generation asks for a miraculous sign!   Christ (Matt. 12:39)

Do not put the Lord your God to the test.

Christ (Matt. 4:7)

If our purpose is to please God, we should not ask for proofs He does not approve:

> ...it is incumbent upon a lowly servant to acquiesce to whatever proof God hath appointed, and not to follow his own idle fancy. If the wishes of the people were to be gratified not a single disbeliever would remain on earth...May God save thee, shouldst thou seek any evidence according to thy selfish desire; rather it behooveth thee to uphold the unfailing proof which God hath appointed. The object of thy belief in God is but to secure His good-pleasure.[55]   The Báb

As the Book of Exodus reports, Aaron performed some incredible miracles, far more difficult than the phenomenon of the empty tomb. "But the magicians did the same thing by their secret arts" (Exodus 8:7). What is the value of a faith that rests on proofs with such a fragile foundation—proofs that can be copied by mere magicians?

Unfortunately, many Christians have built their faith entirely on miracles. While traveling in India, I encountered several cults who attributed astonishing miracles to their leaders. Should we accept those cults by such evidence?

In a TV sermon, a famous Christian leader recently said, "Christ has risen! That is the most important fact in human history. The Christian Faith stands or falls on the resurrection of Jesus Christ." Some Christians do not believe in *physical* resurrection of Jesus, among them is a distinguished biblical scholar,

Bishop John Spong, who has written a book titled *Resurrection: Myth or Reality?* to disprove it. Is it fitting to build a great religion on a miracle that even some of its devoted and distinguished supporters deny?

The question is not whether Jesus rose from the dead. ***He had the power to raise not only Himself but all the peoples of the earth***. He was, as Bahá'u'lláh calls Him, "the Lord of the visible and the invisible." And as He Himself declares, "All authority has been given to Me in heaven and on earth" (Matt. 28:18). The question is this: Is it dignified and credible to base the evidence of the One who has transformed our planet for 2,000 years, and created one of the greatest civilizations the world has ever seen, on an empty tomb? No, the greatness of Christ does not lie in rolling a stone and rising from a tomb, but in His celestial powers to raise a sublime civilization and to lift the hearts and minds of countless millions of spiritually starving and dead to an abundant and everlasting life.

By glorifying miracles, we put a weapon into the hand of every impostor, every cult leader, every deceiver who can manipulate gullible people with a long list of testimonials to his astonishing and miraculous powers.

No, the greatness of Christ does not lie in reviving a body but in restoring the souls of millions for centuries. The evidence of His greatness must be sought in His supreme love and sacrifice, in His character, in His faith, and in the wondrous fruits He brought forth. No one can claim a knowledge and wisdom equal to His, no one can bring forth fruits as fragrant and nourishing as His.

Jim says, "I am the greatest man in the world." "What makes you so great?" Sally asks. "Look," Jim says, "I can lift a truck with one arm." "Does that make you the greatest man?" Sally asks. "Yes," Jim responds, "no one else can do it."

A mighty arm is no proof of greatness. Before the astonished eyes of millions of people, the famous magician David Copperfield caused the Statue of Liberty to disappear. He also caused a train surrounded by people holding hands to suddenly vanish. Do these achievements make him a great man? Only a great magician, and no more.

Aside from this, all those who wrote or left records of the resurrection were believers and sympathizers. Would a jury be able to come to a convincing decision simply by the word of sympathizers? And if they did, how credible would it be to people living 2,000 years later?

Bahá'u'lláh and the Báb both performed numerous miracles that are well-documented. Yet the Bahá'ís refer to them only historically, and not as evidence.

The purpose of showing the irrelevance of miracles to the mission of Messengers is not to undermine the faith of the believers, many of whom have been taught to base their beliefs primarily on demonstrations of miraculous powers by their Savior and Redeemer, *but rather to strengthen their faith and devotion. Recognizing the true standards by which God's Messengers distinguish themselves will only validate our beliefs*. It will shift our faith from shaky ground to a firm foundation. It will move the evidence from the world of magic to the world of meaning. It will raise the evidence of divine

Mission to such supreme heights that no cult leader, no magician, no impostor, no deceiver can ever approach.

Under future topics, we will study the true standards of divine mission again. As we shall see, those standards are infinitely more reasonable and reliable than that of miraculous records.

If miracles are not proofs, then what purpose do they serve? Only this purpose: They can awaken the truth seekers. People will say, "If someone is capable of doing these wonders, maybe I should look into his claim." If used for this purpose, miracles serve a positive function: They awaken and move the slumbering masses to investigate the truth.

We are all attracted and impressed by the glamour of the magical and the miraculous. The popularity of magic throughout history is an evidence of this. As long as we use miracles for inspiration and motivation, we have not done wrong. ***It is the abuse that must be avoided***.

By What Evidence Did Christ Prove His Divine Station?

...Christ, solitary and alone, without a helper or protector, without armies and legions, and under the greatest oppression, uplifted the standard of God before all the people of the world, and withstood them, and finally conquered all, although outwardly He was crucified. Now this is a veritable miracle which can never be denied. There is no need of any other proof of the truth of Christ.[56]

'Abdu'l-Bahá

The following piece, widely quoted in Christian publications, expresses the two most significant evidences for Christ—***Himself*** and ***His profound influence on humankind***:

Who was Christ?

Here is a man
who was born of Jewish parents,
the child of a peasant woman...
He never wrote a book.
He never held an office.
He never owned a home.
He never had a family.
He never went to college.
He never put foot inside a big city.
He never traveled two hundred
miles from the place
where he was born.
He never did one of the things
that usually accompany greatness.
He had no credentials
but himself...

What difference did He make?

Twenty wide centuries
have come and gone,
and he is the centerpiece
of the human race and the
leader of the column of progress.
I am far within the mark
when I say that all the armies
that ever marched,
and all the navies
that were ever built,

have not affected the life of man
upon earth
as powerfully as has that
One Solitary Life.

The statement was written by a Christian author about Christ, but the fundamental principle it contains— a humble person shaping lives for thousands of years—applies to all the great Messengers, for they are, indeed, one: They draw their power from a single Source. Consider this example: Does not the statement—who was Christ, and what difference did He make?—apply equally to Muhammad, the One who came after Christ? American historian Michael Hart has published a book specifically about the hundred most influential figures in history.[57] He puts Muhammad's name—the misrepresented Messenger in the West—at the top of his list. His main reason is that Muhammad not only exerted spiritual power over the lives of His followers, but also established a political system based on His teachings. How is it possible for such a Figure who, as testified by historians, could hardly read and write to exert such a power without God's aid, to establish such a vast civilization without His blessings? A forthcoming book of mine—*The Spirit That Acknowledged Jesus Christ*—presents an astonishing similarity between the teachings of Christ and Muhammad.

Let us consider one prominent Christian and see why He believes in Christ. Dr. James Kennedy is among the most highly respected Christian scholars and orators of our time. He has expressed special interest in reason as a means of understanding and proving religion. He states:

> The Bible never calls us to blind faith but always to a faith in those things that have been established by evidence.[58]

Dr. Kennedy has published a book titled *Why I Believe*, which is widely distributed. In the book he has a chapter titled, "Why I Believe in Christ" in which he demonstrates that the life and character of Christ clearly point to His divine station and mission. In another chapter called, "Why I Believe in Christianity," he considers the transforming power of Christ over the lives of countless millions as sufficient evidence of the faith He established. Dr. Kennedy considers the most essential evidence for Christ to be ***His life and character*** and ***His transforming influence over the destiny of our planet***. In his other works, he adds the fulfillment of prophecies as another critical evidence.

If we put all the words of Jesus together, it would make only a small book, but what a power that small book has exerted on humankind.

> The grass withers and the flowers fall, but the word of our God stands forever.   Isaiah 40:8

Just by looking at Christ's words and deeds, we can clearly discern His distinction. His words were powerful yet gentle. They expressed supreme love, courage, wisdom, compassion, forgiveness, and self-sacrifice. Then, by His deeds, He proved what He meant. His enduring influence came from both His words and His deeds:

> He [Christ] was a prophet, ***powerful in word and deed*** before God and all the people.   Luke 24:19

How could a seemingly ordinary person from a poor family make so much difference?

> That mighty Jewish nation toppled and crumbled away, but those few souls who sought shelter beneath the Messianic Tree [Christianity] transformed all human life.[59]   'Abdu'l-Bahá

Those who regard Jesus Himself as the essential evidence can never be disappointed, for His thoughts, His words, and His deeds are clearly distinct and distinguished. An ordinary person can in no way compete with His excellence. Is the proof of the sun in its light and glory, or in some records left by previous observers? Which is more reliable?

In his classic work *Caesar and Christ*, historian Will Durant states:

> That a few simple men should in one generation have invented so powerful and appealing a personality, so lofty an ethic and so inspiring a vision of human brotherhood, would be a miracle far more incredible than any recorded in the Gospels. After two centuries of Higher Criticism the outlines of the life, character, and teaching of Christ, remain reasonably clear, and constitute the most fascinating feature in the history of Western man.[60]

In our search for truth, instead of following our own fantasies, illusions, and assumptions, we should submit to God's standards:

O friend! It behooveth us not to waive the injunction of God, but rather acquiesce and submit to that which He hath ordained as His divine Testimony.[61]   Bahá'u'lláh

Say: The first and foremost testimony establishing His truth is His own Self. Next to this testimony is His Revelation.[62]   Bahá'u'lláh

Christ never said "Ye shall know God's Messengers by their miracles," yet that is what most people do. He *did* say, "Ye shall know them by their fruits," yet that is what most people do not do.

What constitutes the evidence of truth? What are the proofs of the One who claims that His Word is the Word of God? Discovering the answers to these questions should be the first and foremost concern of every seeker of truth.

Bahá'u'lláh proclaims repeatedly, as did Christ and other great Messengers, that He speaks only the Word of God, that He teaches nothing from Himself. Should we accept His claim without seeking evidence?

When God sends a Messenger, He endows Him with distinctions that no other human being can copy. He makes Him shine as brightly as the sun with peerless glory and splendor. Otherwise, how could anyone be accountable for denying Him? How could anyone be accountable for following falsehood, for choosing an impostor? The question of proof is so vital, it will be examined again and again under various headings in this and the next volume.

The first and foremost evidence that distinguishes the divine from the deceptive is the life of the One

who advances a claim. That will be our next topic
of study. First, we will examine the life of the Báb,
the Herald of the Bahá'í Faith, and then the life of
Bahá'u'lláh, its Founder. Later, we will study the
second most significant standard of distinction: the
Revelation that a Messenger brings, the teachings
He reveals, and His impact on both the individual
and society. The third most significant standard of
distinction is the fulfillment of all prophecies in
sacred Scriptures about the One who makes a
claim. That standard will also be examined, but
only briefly, in this book.

Who Was the Báb?

By studying the life and words of the Báb, we can
discover every proof that God has bestowed on His
great Messengers and Redeemers:

> Thou art the Repository of all Our proofs in this
> Day.[63]   The Báb

On May 22, 1844, a young man who called Himself the Báb (the Gate) proclaimed Himself the One
promised in all Holy Scriptures. He declared the
dawning of a new day in the religious history of
humankind: the day of peace and unity, the age of
the coming of the heavenly Kingdom to the earthly,
the day of divine justice. Here is an invitation from
the Báb to all seekers and lovers of truth:

> Assuredly we are today living in the Days of
> God. These are the glorious days on the like of
> which the sun hath never risen in the past. These
> are the days which the people in bygone times

eagerly expected. What hath then befallen you that ye are fast asleep? These are the days wherein God hath caused the Day-Star of Truth to shine resplendent. What hath then caused you to keep your silence? These are the appointed days which ye have been yearningly awaiting in the past—the days of the advent of divine justice.[64]

The Báb

Just as John the Baptist foretold the coming of One greater than Himself, so did the Báb. He referred to One still to come by many titles, among them ***Bahá'u'lláh*** (Glory of God).

The Báb came from southern Persia, where God promised to set His throne. Within the brief span of His ministry (1844-1850), He attracted many follow-ers, thousands of whom were massacred, mostly by order of fanatical religious leaders of Islam who feared the loss of their powers. The Báb Himself was imprisoned and finally executed in 1850.

The Báb's mission was primarily symbolic of the destruction of the old order; Bahá'u'lláh's mission was the creation of a new order to replace the old. One came to clear the way, the other to build.

All God's Messengers reveal the same signs of great-ness. They manifest His light with full glory and splendor. If we know what a genuine diamond is like, we can use our knowledge to test and identify other diamonds. Otherwise, we may consider a diamond a stone and a stone a diamond. Therefore we need standards. The best way we can find the standards is to look at the lives of God's great Messengers to identify what makes them stand out from others.

The lives of Jesus and the Báb are astonishingly alike. *Lord of Lords* by this author presents 83 parallels between the lives, the works, and the destinies of these two great Redeemers.

How Was the Báb Martyred?

The good shepherd gives his life for the sheep.
Christ (John 10:11)

The Son of Man came not to be ministered unto, but to minister, and to give His life...
Christ (Matt. 20:28)

I have sacrificed myself wholly for Thee; I have accepted curses for Thy sake, and have yearned for naught but martyrdom in the path of Thy love. Sufficient witness unto me is God, the Exalted, the Protector, the Ancient of Days.[65]   The Báb

I heard a Voice calling in my inmost being: "Do thou sacrifice the thing which Thou lovest most in the path of God..."[66]   The Báb

For assuredly *whatsoever God hath decreed for Me shall come to pass* and naught else save that which God hath ordained for us shall ever touch us. *Woe betide him from whose hands floweth evil*, and blessed the man from whose hands floweth good.[67]   The Báb

Woe to the world because of the things that cause people to sin! *Such things must come, but woe to the man through whom they come*!
Christ (Matt. 18:7)

The Báb was martyred in July of 1850, a few months short of His 31st birthday. His martyrdom is one of the best documented and most incredible events in religious history. It was observed by an estimated audience of 10,000 and recorded by writers of various religious persuasions, and even by the official historian of the state that ordered the execution.

First, a few words regarding the reasons behind the martyrdom. Why did Christ and the Báb offer their lives? An essential feature of the design of creation is that every worthy achievement must be preceded or accompanied by a sacrifice. Whether it is raising well-behaved children, getting a degree, staying healthy, losing weight, or eliminating racism, sexism, and poverty, some degree of sacrifice is required.

To grow and multiply, to bear flowers and fruits, the seed must sacrifice itself:

> Unless a kernel of wheat falls to the ground and dies, it remains only a single seed. But if it dies, it produces many seeds.   Christ (John 12:24)

What is by far the greatest achievement? It is educating humanity, elevating the human spirit to everlasting hope and happiness; it is leading the soul from the kingdom of earth to the Kingdom of Heaven. Can such a glorious purpose be achieved without sacrifice?

Human beings are best inspired by models who show their devotion and sincerity through examples. The first ones to offer perfect examples of devotion, nobility, and self-sacrifice are God's chosen Messengers. If they, with all their perfections and powers, submitted themselves to the law of sacrifice, are we not inspired to do the same?

I have set you an example: you are to do as I have done for you. Christ (John 13:15)

I am the good shepherd; the good shepherd giveth his life for the sheep. Christ (John 10:11)

To most of us, self-sacrifice has negative connotations. It implies giving something away. That is a misconception. Self-sacrifice involves no loss; it is the process by which short-term interests are exchanged for long-term dividends. It is like exchanging junk bonds for reliable and late-maturing bonds, or junk food for healthy food. Self-sacrifice is the catalyzer of perfection; it is the yeast that elevates the human spirit by breaking down apathy, inertia, complacency, pride, self-glory, and attachment to the world. It is the price that must be paid for a lasting and genuine happiness.

God's ways are often opposite to ours. By His standard, "We must lose to gain; we must give to obtain; we must be humble to be exalted; we must be least to be greatest; we must die to live."

...how can My way accord with thine?[68]

Bahá'u'lláh

Behold how contrary are the ways of the Manifestations of God, as ordained by the King of creation, to the ways and desires of men![69]

Bahá'u'lláh

All great Messengers have endured pain and suffering. The only difference is this: Some of them have become martyrs, others *living* martyrs. Death does not necessarily impose the gravest suffering. In some ways, life can be far more painful than death.

Bahá'u'lláh's life was of this kind. Martyrdom attracts our attention because, in addition to being tragic, it is dramatic. The deaths of Christ and the Báb were of this kind.

In the Báb's death we can discern evidence of a divine power at work. Should we use that evidence as proof of His station? Definitely not. Then what purpose should it serve? Only this: *It should elevate us from apathy to awareness. It is not evidence in itself, but a call for us to investigate the evidence.* For instance, you know you will be asleep at 7:00 a.m. You set your clock to awaken you at that time to be ready for an invited guest. In the state of sleep, you are unaware of the coming of the guest. *When you awaken, you begin to see and hear. That is the only purpose miracles should serve.* You do not welcome your guest because of the alarm clock, you welcome him because you see him and recognize him with your own eyes.

With these points in mind, let us proceed with the story of the Báb's martyrdom. The Persian government wanted to make the execution of the Báb a lesson to all people, especially to His followers. Hence, a decision was made to make it a public event. But, as we shall see, God had a different plan.

Just before the time of the execution, the Báb was in prison speaking to a disciple. A government official came to the Báb's prison cell and told Him to come to the public square for the impending execution. The Báb asked for a little time to finish His conversation with the disciple, but the official would not comply. The Báb offered this warning: "Not until I have said to him all those things that I wish to say, can any earthly power silence Me. Though all the world be armed against Me, yet shall they be powerless to deter Me from fulfilling, to the last word, My intention."[70] The official ignored the warning and took the Báb (along with a young disciple who wanted to die with Him) to the public square to be shot by a regiment of 750 soldiers, who stood in three lines ready to fire.

The regiment was headed by an Armenian colonel, Sám Khán, who had no animosity toward the Báb and no interest in executing two young men for their religious beliefs. To absolve himself of responsibility, he went to the Báb and said, "I profess the Christian Faith and entertain no ill will against you. If your Cause be the Cause of Truth, enable me to free myself from the obligation to shed your blood."[71]

The Báb replied, "Follow your instructions, and if your intention be sincere, the Almighty is surely able to relieve you from your perplexity."[72]

The martyrdom of the Báb and His disciple was planned with precision. To give people a good view of the event, the officials suspended the Báb and His disciple above the ground by putting two heavy ropes under their armpits and tying the ropes to a heavy nail driven into a thick wall. The Báb's disciple pleaded to be placed in such a position that his body would shield that of his Master. He was suspended so that his head rested on his Master's chest.

At about 10:00 a.m., the gaze of thousands of onlookers was fixed on the two young men suspended in the air. The first of the three lines of soldiers,

250 of them, were ordered to fire. They fired, then knelt so that the second and then the third lines of soldiers could fire. The firing of 750 bullets created a great cloud of smoke that obscured the people's vision. (The smoke came from the gun powder used in those days.) For a few minutes, people were blinded, but when the smoke cleared, they saw no trace of the Báb. His disciple was standing unharmed on the ground just below the point of suspension.

It is hard to imagine the uproar, the astonishment, and the confusion that seized the onlookers, especially the government officials. The nervous and puzzled officials frantically searched for the Báb. Where do you think He was found? In His original prison cell, completing His unfinished conversation with His disciple.

The man who located Him was the same man who had taken Him for execution. When he arrived, the Báb was ready. His face radiated with unruffled calm. He welcomed the official by saying, "Now you may proceed to fulfill your intention."[73] The guard was so shaken by what he saw that he refused to take the Báb a second time. He left the scene and resigned from his position.

In the meantime, the Christian colonel, who had been looking for any reason to excuse himself from the ominous task, could not have been more jubilant. He saw this as a sure sign from God and immediately withdrew his soldiers and swore never again to engage in that task, even if his refusal led to his death.

A second regiment was ordered into action. Now two hours had passed. It was about noon. Because of the seemingly miraculous event, the Báb had a more receptive audience. He had a chance to address the people:

> Had you believed in Me, O wayward generation, every one of you would have followed the example of this youth [the disciple who wanted to die with Him]...The day will come when you will have recognized Me; that day I shall have ceased to be with you.[74]

Everything was now ready. The second regiment took position and was ordered to fire. This time the bullets reached their targets. The two bodies were so shattered and riddled with bullets, they blended into one mass of mangled flesh and bone, except for the face of the Báb, which miraculously remained intact.

> Unto God do I commit Mine affair...Naught shall touch Me besides that which God, My Lord, hath pre-ordained for Me. In Him have I placed My whole trust...[75]
> The Báb

> I am well pleased to lay down My life in Thy path and ere long to return to Thy presence. Unto Thee be praise in the heavens and on the earth.[76]
> The Báb

> Glory be unto Thee, O my God. Thou art well aware that I have proclaimed Thy Word and have not failed in the mission Thou didst enjoin upon me.[77]
> The Báb

> I, verily, have not fallen short of My duty to admonish...people, and to devise means whereby they may turn towards God, their Lord, and believe in God, their Creator.[78]
> The Báb

The One called the Desire of nations, the Savior and Redeemer of humankind, Lord of Lords and King of Kings, was made a sacrifice for the world. This is the way it has been and may always be:

> You always resist the Holy Spirit! Was there ever a prophet your fathers did not persecute? They even killed those who predicted the coming of the Righteous One. Acts 7:51-52

> Great spirits have always encountered opposition from mediocre minds. Albert Einstein

The sacrifices made by the Báb and Jesus present us with two dramatic examples by which God teaches us lessons of detachment and dedication. He allows the Ones He loves most to become sacrificial Lambs. The few examples of self-sacrifice by God's chosen Messengers have had and will continue to have far more influence in elevating the human spirit than countless books of commandments and counsels.

How did this seemingly incredible event happen? The only explanation offered is that some bullets hit the rope first and severed it, thus allowing the Báb and His disciple to fall to the ground. Did God intervene or was it merely a coincidence? We have the choice to come to either conclusion.

Who Was Bahá'u'lláh?

In examining the evidence for the One who has claimed to speak the Word of God, the most vital questions are these: Who was He? What was He like? How did He live? What happened to Him?

Here are a few features of Bahá'u'lláh's life, adapted mostly from a book titled *Some Answered Questions*:

Bahá'u'lláh was born in 1817, in Persia, to a rich and noble family. He died in 1892, as a prisoner and exile in the Holy Land. As an infant, He astonished His parents by His uniqueness and distinctions. His father related that He would never cry or scream. "You don't know," he said, "what a potential He has, how intelligent He is! He is like a flame of fire, and in His tender years superior to young people."[79] Bahá'u'lláh's father was so infatuated with Him that he wrote a piece of poetry in his son's honor, inscribed it on a plaque, and hung it on the wall of a summer mansion in which Bahá'u'lláh lived. The content of the poetry shows that the father sensed the divine destiny of his Son:

> When thou enterest the sacred abode of the Beloved say:
> "I am at thy command.
> This is the home of love; enter with reverence.
> This is holy ground; remove thy shoes when thou enterest here."[80]

People were attracted by Bahá'u'lláh's many distinctions. He did not attend any school, yet astonished people by His wisdom and knowledge. Even His enemies testified to His greatness. Great thinkers flocked to His presence, asking their most difficult questions. They said, "This man is unique in all perfections."

> He had an extraordinary power of attraction, which was felt by all. People always crowded around Him. Ministers and people of the Court

would surround Him, and the children also were devoted to Him. When He was only thirteen or fourteen years old He became renowned for His learning. He would converse on any subject and solve any problem presented to Him. In large gatherings He would discuss matters with the 'Ulamá (religious leaders) and would explain intricate religious questions. All of them used to listen to Him with the greatest interest.[81]

He showed no interest in politics:

When Bahá'u'lláh was twenty-two years old, His father died, and the Government wished Him to succeed to His father's position in the Ministry, as was customary in Persia, but Bahá'u'lláh did not accept the offer. Then the Prime Minister said: "Leave him to himself. Such a position is unworthy of him. He has some higher aim in view. I cannot understand him, but I am convinced that he is destined for some lofty career. His thoughts are not like ours. Let him alone."[82]

Bahá'u'lláh was known especially for His generosity and love for the poor:

He was most generous, giving abundantly to the poor. None who came to Him were turned away. The doors of His house were open to all. He always had many guests. This unbounded generosity was conducive to greater astonishment from the fact that He sought neither position nor prominence.[83]

One day Bahá'u'lláh sent 'Abdu'l-Bahá, His eldest Son, to inspect the work of the shepherds who were taking care of His sheep. 'Abdu'l-Bahá was a small child at the time, and the persecutions against Bahá'u'lláh and His family had not yet started. Bahá'u'lláh then had a good deal of land in the mountains and owned large herds of sheep. When the inspection was finished and 'Abdu'l-Bahá was ready to leave, the man who had accompanied Him said, "It is your father's custom to leave a gift for each shepherd." 'Abdu'l-Bahá became silent for a while, because He did not have anything to give them. The man, however, insisted that the shepherds were expecting something. Then 'Abdu'l-Bahá had an idea that made Him very happy! He would give the shepherds the sheep they were taking care of! Bahá'u'lláh was very much pleased when He heard about 'Abdu'l-Bahá's generous thoughts towards the shepherds. He humorously remarked that everyone had better take good care of 'Abdu'l-Bahá because someday He would give Himself away. Of course, this is exactly what 'Abdu'l-Bahá did for the rest of His life. He gave everything He had, each and every moment of His life, to humanity, to unite us and bring us true happiness.[84]

Bahá'u'lláh was also known for His courage to stand against the powerful who would abuse their power:

All classes of men marveled at His miraculous success in emerging unscathed from the most perilous encounters. Nothing short of Divine protection, they thought, could have ensured His safety on such occasions. Not once did Bahá'u'lláh, beset though He was by the gravest perils, submit to the arrogance, the greed and the treachery of those around Him. In His constant association, during those days, with the highest dignitaries of the realm, whether ecclesiastical or State officials, He was never content simply to accede to the views they expressed or the claims they advanced. He would, at their gatherings, fearlessly champion the cause of truth, would assert the rights of the downtrodden, defending the weak and protecting the innocent.[85]

Bahá'u'lláh spent the early part of His life in the utmost joy and happiness. But because of His beliefs, He became a target of prejudice and persecution. Thousands of fanatical believers rose against Him. Religious leaders were terrified of losing their power. They said, "This man intends to destroy religion, law, the nation, and the empire." (People made the same accusations against Jesus.) He faced His enemies with the utmost courage, showing no weakness or fear.

Bahá'u'lláh endured almost 40 years of imprisonment and exile, yet He never complained. No human being can imagine what He went through. Among His sufferings was imprisonment in an infamous dungeon in Tihrán, known as the Black Pit or Black Dungeon, where He was kept for four months. In that dungeon He endured and willingly submitted to every conceivable pain and anguish:

- *Total darkness*: The underground prison had neither lights nor windows.

- *A terrible stench*: About 150 of the worst criminals were thrown in that dark, deep, damp dungeon with no air circulation or sanitary facilities. The ground was covered with several inches of filthy mud and mire.

- *Hunger and thirst*: For the first three days and nights Bahá'u'lláh received neither food nor water.

- *Severe pain and lack of mobility*: Bahá'u'lláh's feet were put in stocks, and on His neck was placed a chain so heavy that He could not hold Himself upright. (To hold the weight of the chain, Bahá'u'lláh had to press His hands against the ground covered with slime up to His wrists. Sometimes they put a support under His chain.) From the weight of the harsh metal, His neck became inflamed and injured.

- *Little if any sleep*: Under those horrible conditions Bahá'u'lláh could hardly sleep.

- *Lack of clothes*: His outer garments were stripped away on His way to the prison.

- *Illness*: Because of the unsanitary conditions and poison put in His food, Bahá'u'lláh suffered grave illness.

- *Homelessness*: All His property was confiscated.

- *Loneliness*: "During this time none of His friends were able to get access to Him."[86]

- *Being surrounded by the worst criminals* who had little if any hope of survival or freedom.

- *Anxiety about His family*: Bahá'u'lláh's family members, including His young children, were at the mercy of fanatical mobs, filled with rage and incited to revenge. (His Son, 'Abdu'l-Bahá, was then 9 years old.)

- *Deep grief and concern for His devoted and distinguished disciples*, who were being hunted down, tortured, and killed by enraged mobs out-side the prison.

- *Concern about the future*: From that prison Bahá'u'lláh was banished to strange lands. As a prophecy foretold (Matthew 25:41-46), He became a stranger (an exile). Never again did He see His homeland.

- *Deep sorrow* for people who were rejecting God's choicest blessings and bounties.

It was in this dungeon that Bahá'u'lláh expressed the first intimations of His Divine Mission:

One night, in a dream, these exalted words were heard on every side: "Verily, We shall render Thee victorious by Thyself and by Thy Pen. Grieve Thou not for that which hath befallen Thee, neither be Thou afraid, for Thou art in safety. Erelong will God raise up the treasures of the earth—men who will aid Thee through Thyself and through Thy Name..."[87]

Bahá'u'lláh stated again and again that He spoke only by God's command, and not of His own choosing:

God is my witness, O people! I was asleep on My couch, when lo, the Breeze of God wafting over Me roused Me from My slumber. His quickening Spirit revived Me, and My tongue was unloosed to voice His call...Think ye, O people, that I hold within My grasp the control of God's ultimate Will and Purpose? Far be it from Me to advance such claim. To this I testify before God, the Almighty, the Exalted, the All-Knowing, the All Wise. Had the ultimate destiny of God's Faith

been in Mine hands, I would have never consented, even though for one moment, to manifest
Myself unto you, nor would I have allowed one
word to fall from My lips. Of this God Himself
is, verily, a witness.[88]

O king! I was but a man like others, asleep
upon My couch, when lo, the breezes of the
All-Glorious were wafted over Me, and taught
Me the knowledge of all that hath been. This
thing is not from Me, but from One Who is
Almighty and All-Knowing...This is but a leaf
which the winds of the will of thy Lord, the
Almighty, the All-Praised, have stirred. Can it be
still when the tempestuous winds are blowing?
Nay, by Him Who is the Lord of all Names and
Attributes![89]

Bahá'u'lláh's arrest and imprisonment in that dungeon
give us only a glimpse of the sufferings He endured
for nearly 40 years in three different countries.
How could anyone survive the scourge of such
unrelenting pressures? How much pain can a human
being endure? Why would God allow the One He
loved the most to go through so much suffering?
Did not Jesus endure similar ordeals? Bahá'u'lláh
refers repeatedly to His afflictions:

Worldly friends, seeking their own good, appear
to love one the other, whereas the true Friend
[Bahá'u'lláh] hath loved and doth love you for
your own sakes; indeed He hath suffered for your
guidance countless afflictions. Be not disloyal to
such a Friend, nay rather hasten unto Him...Open
your ears that ye may hearken unto the word of
God, the help in peril, the self-existent.[90]

The religious leaders feared Bahá'u'lláh's influence, so they had Him exiled to another land. They thought in a strange land His influence would die out. But His charm captivated many more disciples. They exiled Him again and again. The results were the same. Finally, they sent Him to the worst place they could find: a prison for murderers and thieves, located in a remote city ('Akká) with a dreadful climate and foul water, a city described as "the metropolis of the owl." The sufferings Bahá'u'lláh endured in 'Akká surpassed even those He experienced in the Black Dungeon.

Bahá'u'lláh was placed in a barren, filthy room, while His followers were crowded into another, the floor of which was covered with mud. Ten soldiers were posted to stand guard over them. To add further to their misery, the exiles, parched from a long day in the hot sun, soon found that the only water available to them was unfit for consumption. Mothers were unable to feed their babies, and infants cried for hours. 'Abdu'l-Bahá appealed repeatedly to the guards and the governor for mercy, but to no avail. The next morning the exiles were given their first daily ration of water and three inedible loaves of salty, coarse, black bread, which they were later allowed to exchange in the market for two loaves of better quality.

Under these conditions, all but 'Abdu'l-Bahá and one other fell ill. Within a matter of days three men died. The officials denied the prisoners permission to leave the citadel to bury them, and the guards demanded payment before removing the bodies. Bahá'u'lláh ordered that His prayer rug, the only item of any value that He possessed, be sold to cover the cost of the burial. The guards pocketed the money and buried the men in the clothes in which they died, without coffins and without washing or wrapping the bodies in shrouds.

Three days after the exiles' arrival, the Sultán's edict was read aloud in the mosque. It sentenced Bahá'u'lláh, His family, and His companions to life imprisonment and expressly forbade the exiles to associate with one another or with local inhabitants. Harsh, indeed, were the terms and conditions that Bahá'u'lláh faced upon His internment in the "afflictive prison" of 'Akká—an internment that marked the culmination of His sufferings.[91]

During Bahá'u'lláh's imprisonment in 'Akká, His young son, "Mírzá Mihdí was pacing the roof, wrapped in devotions, when he fell through a skylight. Mortally wounded, his dying wish to his Father was that his life might be a ransom for those who were prevented from attaining Bahá'u'lláh's presence."[92] In a prayer, Bahá'u'lláh speaks of the sacrifice of His son:

I have, O my Lord, offered up that which Thou hast given Me, that Thy servants may be quickened, and all that dwell on earth be united.[93]

Here Bahá'u'lláh explains why He accepted so much pain and suffering:

The Ancient Beauty [Bahá'u'lláh] hath consented to be bound with chains that mankind may be released from its bondage, and hath accepted to be made a prisoner within this most mighty Stronghold that the whole world may attain unto true liberty. He hath drained to its dregs the cup of sorrow, that all the peoples of the earth may attain unto abiding joy, and be filled with gladness. This is of the mercy of your Lord, the Compassionate, the Most Merciful. We have accepted to be abased, O believers in the Unity of God, that ye may be exalted, and have suffered manifold afflictions, that ye might prosper and flourish. He Who hath come to build anew the whole world, behold, how they...have forced Him to dwell within the most desolate of cities![94]

In spite of this severe repression, Bahá'u'lláh's influence continued to spread, His glory became more evident. From behind prison walls, He triumphed over all His enemies.

For if this idea...is of human origin, it will collapse; but if it is from God, you will never be able to put them [the believers] down, and you risk finding yourself at war with God.

Acts 5:38-39

When Bahá'u'lláh was exiled to the Holy Land, those aware of biblical prophecies suddenly realized what had happened: Bahá'u'lláh's enemies had, unknowingly, become the very instruments for the fulfillment of prophecies about Him. For the Bible predicts repeatedly that the Redeemer of the Last Days will come to the Holy Land. Those who had wished to destroy Him became the means of His triumph. (For a list of these prophecies and many others, see *Lord of Lords*, and *King of Kings*.)

While under arrest in 1868, Bahá'u'lláh addressed the kings and rulers of the earth, asking them to act with justice and to work for peace. With one exception, they ignored His call. He predicted their downfall and His own triumph.

Among these sovereigns was Napoleon III. Bahá'u'lláh asked him to investigate why He was in prison. The sovereign did not respond. Bahá'u'lláh sent a second letter, predicting his downfall. Soon thereafter, in 1870, war between Germany and France broke out. Everything seemed to be in Napoleon's favor, yet he was defeated, dishonored, and debased. Other sovereigns addressed by Bahá'u'lláh encountered similar fates. Every prediction that Bahá'u'lláh made came true. These are discussed in a book titled ***The Prisoner and the King***, by William Sears.

Bahá'u'lláh's greatness touched even those who did not follow Him. They wrote about His knowledge, His kindness, and His patience. They flocked to His presence and marveled at His wondrous works.

How often would one of His bitter enemies say to himself, "When I see Him, I will argue with Him and defeat Him in this way..." But when faced with Bahá'u'lláh, he would find himself speechless, unable to utter a word.

Bahá'u'lláh declared His willingness to be tested. No other Messenger has ever consented to prove Himself by miracles. To leave them with no excuse, Bahá'u'lláh said that He was willing to perform any miracle that the religious leaders asked. The only condition He set was that, after the miracle was performed, they would acknowledge the validity of

His claim. The religious leaders declined to accept the condition. (God has always been against proving Himself by miracles, see Matt. 7:4. We cannot be sure why Bahá'u'lláh accepted this request. Perhaps one reason was that He knew it would be rejected.)

Bahá'u'lláh showed His dependence on the divine and detachment from worldly desires by associating with the poor and the humble and avoiding the powerful and the pompous.[95] A curious prince wanted to meet Bahá'u'lláh. But to be seen with Him meant danger. He sent a message asking to meet with Him secretly. In response, Bahá'u'lláh sent him a piece of poetry to this effect: "Unless you have a desire to sacrifice your life, don't come here. This is the way if you wish to meet Bahá. If you are unprepared for this journey, don't come, and don't bring trouble." The prince could not take the chance and declined.

For nearly 50 years Bahá'u'lláh faced bitter enemies who killed thousands of His followers yet failed to destroy Him. Repeatedly they planned and plotted against Him, but to no avail.

Are these marks of distinction not similar to those found in the life of Jesus?

> We must be just and acknowledge what an Educator this Glorious Being was, what marvelous signs were manifested by Him, and what power and might have been realized in the world through Him.[96]
>   'Abdu'l-Bahá

> My deeds done in my Father's name are my credentials.
>   Christ (John 10:25)

Accept the evidence of my deeds.

Christ (John 10:38)

What Station Does Bahá'u'lláh Claim?

Prophecies indicate that at "the end of the age" a universal Redeemer will come to unify all the religions and peoples of the earth under one God and one faith. He will establish righteousness, peace, and justice:

The desired of all nations shall come...

Haggai 2:7

Lo, the Desired One is come with manifest dominion![97]

Bahá'u'lláh

Justice will dwell in the desert and righteousness live in the fertile field. The fruit of righteousness will be peace; the effect of righteousness will be quietness and confidence forever. My people will live in peaceful dwelling places, in secure homes, in undisturbed places of rest...how blessed you will be.

Isaiah 32:16-20

Bahá'u'lláh claims to be that universal Redeemer and unifier of the human race, the One expected and desired by all nations, the One who will bring righteousness, justice, peace, and prosperity.

Bahá'u'lláh proclaimed His mission in Epistles addressed to common people and to the political and religious leaders. These Epistles have been published under the title *The Proclamation of Bahá'u'lláh*. Here is a brief passage from an Epistle addressed to the kings; ponder the power and authority with which Bahá'u'lláh speaks:

Ye are but vassals, O Kings of the earth! He Who is the King of Kings hath appeared, arrayed in His most wondrous glory, and is summoning you unto Himself, the Help in Peril, the Self-Subsisting. Take heed lest pride deter you from recognizing the Source of Revelation; lest the things of this world shut you out as by a veil from Him Who is the Creator of heaven. Arise, and serve Him Who is the Desire of all nations, Who hath created you through a word from Him, and ordained you to be, for all time, the emblems of His sovereignty...

Forsake your palaces, and haste ye to gain admittance into His Kingdom. This, indeed, will profit you both in this world and in the next. To this testifieth the Lord of the realm on high, did ye but know it.[98]

Bahá'u'lláh proclaims in the clearest, most certain, and most emphatic terms His station as the supreme Savior and Redeemer of the World, the Promised One of all ages and religions, *the return of Christ* to Christians, and *the Glory of the Lord* to the followers of both the Torah and the Gospel. He claims a station referred to throughout the Scriptures as *the Return of the Son in the Glory of His Father, the Lord of the Vineyard, the King of Glory, the Desire of all Nations, the Comforter, the Counselor, and the Prince of Peace.*[99]

The followers of all great faiths expect a World-Redeemer who at the last hour will bring peace and prosperity to our planet. Zoroastrians refer to Him as "Sháh-Bahrám," Buddhists as "the Buddha of universal fellowship," the Hindus as "the Most Great Spirit." The Qur'án calls Him "the Great Announcement."[100] Bahá'u'lláh declared that He fulfilled all these expectations and prophecies.

Here are still more examples of the language and the manner in which Bahá'u'lláh declares His divine mission:

> He who is the Desired One is come in His transcendent majesty...Better is this for you than all ye possess.[101]

> The Hour which We had concealed from the knowledge of the peoples of the earth...hath come to pass.[102]

> He that was hidden from mortal eyes is come! His all-conquering sovereignty is manifest; His all-encompassing splendor is revealed. Beware lest thou hesitate or halt.[103]

> This is the changeless Faith of God, eternal in the past, eternal in the future. Let him that seeketh, attain it; and as to him that hath refused to seek it—verily, God is Self-Sufficient, above any need of His creatures.[104]

> By the righteousness of the Almighty! Every hidden thing hath been manifested through the power of truth. All the favors of God have been sent down, as a token of His grace. The waters of everlasting life have, in their fullness, been proffered unto men. Every single cup hath been borne round by the hand of the Well-Beloved. Draw near, and tarry not, though it be for one short moment.[105]

Verily I say, this is the Day in which mankind can behold the Face, and hear the Voice, of the Promised One...It behoveth every man to blot out the trace of every idle word from the tablet of his heart, and to gaze, with an open and unbiased mind, on the signs of His Revelation, the proofs of His Mission, and the tokens of His glory...

The most grievous veil hath shut out the peoples of the earth from His glory, and hindered them from hearkening to His call. God grant that the light of unity may envelop the whole earth.[106]

Many Christians simply assume that Christ must come with His original name. *King of Kings* presents many prophecies that point to a new name and specifically to *the Glory of God*, which is the English translation of *Bahá'u'lláh*. For instance, the following prophecy from Isaiah points not only to rejection of the Redeemer of our time but also to a new name given to His servants or followers:

I called and you did not answer, I spoke and you did not listen; and you did what was wrong in my eyes and you chose what was against my will. Therefore these are the words of the Lord God: My servants shall eat but you shall starve; my servants shall drink but you shall go thirsty; my servants shall rejoice but you shall be put to shame; my servants shall shout in triumph in the gladness of their hearts, but you shall cry from sorrow and wail from anguish of spirit...the Lord God shall give you over to death; but *his servants he shall call by another name*.   Isaiah 65:12-15

The Book of Revelation also points to a new name:

> Him who overcomes...I will also write on him
> my *new name*.   Revelation 3:12

> To him who overcomes...I will also give him a
> white stone with *a new name* written on it.
>   Revelation 2:17

Christ said that He will come "in His Father's
glory" (Mark 8:38). Since "Father" equals "God,"
"Father's glory" equals "God's Glory," or "Glory
of God," which is the meaning of the word
"Bahá'u'lláh."

In His Epistle to Christians, Bahá'u'lláh declares
Himself the One promised to come in the station
of the Father:

> He Who is the Desired One is come in His tran-
> scendent majesty. Say, Lo! The Father is come,
> and that which ye were promised in the Kingdom
> is fulfilled! This is the Word which the Son
> [Christ] concealed, when to those around Him He
> said: 'Ye cannot bear it now.' And when the
> appointed time was fulfilled and the Hour had
> struck, the Word shone forth above the horizon
> of the Will of God. Beware, O followers of the
> Son, that ye cast it not behind your backs. Take
> ye fast hold of it. Better is this for you than all
> that ye possess. Verily He is nigh unto them that
> do good. The Hour which We had concealed
> from the knowledge of the peoples of the earth
> and of the favored angels hath come to pass. Say,
> verily, He [Christ] hath testified of Me, and I do
> testify of Him.[107]

The coming of a divine Being named "the Glory of God," which is the equivalent of "Bahá'u'lláh," is repeated throughout the Bible, yet it is seldom noticed:

> As truly as I live, all the earth shall be filled with *the glory of the Lord*.   Numbers 14:21

> They will see *the glory of the Lord*, the splendor of our God.   Isaiah 35:2

> Did I not tell you that if you have faith you will see *the glory of God*?   Christ (John 11:40)

> ...he shall come in his own glory and in his Father's.   Christ (Luke 9:26)

> When the Lord...shall appear in his glory.
> Psalms 102:16

> The Lord is come in his great glory.[108]
> Bahá'u'lláh

In His Epistle to Christians, Bahá'u'lláh asks why they allow the name Bahá'u'lláh to stand as an obstacle in testing His claim. He reminds them that the people to whom Jesus was sent prayed constantly for their Redeemer's advent. They expressed the deepest desire to meet Him. Yet when He came, only a few among them, mostly from the disfavored classes of society—the poor and the powerless, the simple and the sinners—recognized His divine glory. Why did their deep love for their adored Redeemer and Master *not* save them from denying Him? They read their Scriptures day and night. Why was their knowledge of no avail to them? Why did their repeated readings of the prophecies *not* guide them to truth?

> You study the scriptures diligently, supposing that in having them you have eternal life; yet, although their testimony points to me, you refuse to come to me for that life.   Christ (John 5:39-40)

Bahá'u'lláh intimates that, without asking these questions and resolving them, we cannot learn from the example of those who were once in our place, of those who thought that by ignoring or opposing Jesus they were doing the right thing, without ever suspecting that they were depriving themselves of the greatest gift that Heaven might bestow upon humans. Without pondering these questions and resolving them, it is extremely difficult, even impossible, to overcome the many obstacles our traditional beliefs place before us. We will be as confused and perplexed as our forebears who repeatedly rejected God's Messengers:

> You always resist the Holy Spirit! Was there ever a prophet your fathers did not persecute? They even killed those who predicted the coming of the Righteous One.   Acts 7:51-52

When you hear the name "Bahá'u'lláh," always remember its meaning: the Glory of God. The human being who lived on earth and called Himself Bahá'u'lláh was simply an instrument for manifesting "the Glory of God" in an earthly temple on an earthly plane. This prayer from Bahá'u'lláh shows His submission and selflessness as a human being before God who created Him and crowned Him with His glory:

Glorified art Thou, O my God! Thou knowest that my sole aim in revealing Thy Cause hath been to reveal Thee and not my self, and to manifest Thy glory rather than my glory. In Thy path, and to attain Thy pleasure, I have scorned rest, joy, delight. At all times and under all conditions my gaze hath been fixed on Thy precepts, and mine eyes bent upon the things Thou hast bidden me observe in Thy Tablets. I have wakened every morning to the light of Thy praise and Thy remembrance, and reached every evening inhaling the fragrances of Thy mercy.[109]

In the following passage, Bahá'u'lláh expresses His humility even before human beings, God's loved ones:

By Thy glory, O Lord of all being, and the Desire of all creation! I would love to lay My face upon every single spot of Thine earth, that perchance it might be honored by touching a spot ennobled by the footsteps of Thy loved ones![110]

What Other Proofs Establish the Validity of Bahá'u'lláh's Station?

- Bahá'u'lláh persisted in His claim to the end, without making the slightest compromise.

- He endured every conceivable adversity, humiliation, and pain for half a century with superhuman resolve, composure, and constancy.

- He revealed Scriptures for 40 years, with no contradictions or changes of mind.

- He spiritualized and raised the ethical standards of millions from every race, creed, and culture.

- He revealed teachings extolled by some of the great thinkers of our time.

- He unified millions of people from diverse races, religions, and cultures.

- He wrote the equivalent of 100 volumes, without research or revision.

- He revealed principles that harmonize religious and scientific truths—a task beyond the reach of the ablest thinkers.

- He fulfilled hundreds of prophecies with perfect precision, in harmony with at least 16 biblical references that pointed to the precise year of the advent of the Báb—the beginning date of the dawning of the new Day: 1844.

- He lived a life pure, divine, and noble, far beyond the reach of any human being.

- He made predictions that have come true.

- He established a Faith that, despite constant and severe persecution, has endured and preserved its unity for a century and a half.

> ***Every plant, which my heavenly Father hath not planted, shall be rooted up.***
>
> Christ (Matt. 15:13)

These are the most reliable proofs—proofs that, unlike miracles, can be tested and verified. Taken together, these 12 distinguishing features set Bahá'u'lláh above impostors; they point to His divine origin. No human being can accomplish such wonders on his own. Only the power of God can allow a person to succeed. They are the main parts of a jigsaw puzzle that only God can design and put together. No piece should be seen alone, apart from the others. Like a tapestry of exquisite beauty and charm, they should be blended and viewed together, every thread in the light of every other. Only then can their divine distinction fully manifest its splendor.

All the preceding points apply equally to the Báb, except for the numbers, such as the duration of His ministry and the number of books He revealed. Thus we have not one, but two supreme Redeemers, each of them manifesting every sign of divine distinction.

God endows His great Messengers and Redeemers with such a distinct spectrum of evidence as no human being can ever produce. He makes their souls shine like the sun among lighted lamps. Is it possible to mistake one for the other? The reason for not seeing the difference has always been and will always be with the beholders, who wear dark veils or try to see the sun through many layers of clouds.

What Station Does the Báb Claim?

O My servants! This is God's appointed Day which the merciful Lord hath promised you in His Book.[111]   The Báb

The station of the Báb is similar to that of Bahá'u'lláh: He was also an independent Messenger, the Founder of a new Faith, with His own Scriptures. Although He expressed absolute humility before Bahá'u'lláh,

He too came in the station of the Lord. That is the honor and title that God bestowed on Him:

> I am the Lamp which the Finger of God hath lit within its niche and caused to shine with death-less splendor. I am the Flame of that supernal Light that glowed upon Sinai...and lay concealed in the midst of the Burning Bush.[112]   The Báb

> O peoples of the earth! Give ear unto God's holy Voice...Whom the Almighty hath graciously chosen for His Own Self. He is indeed none other than the True One, Whom God hath entrusted with this Mission from the midst of the Burning Bush.[113]
> The Báb

> Verily this is none other than the sovereign Truth; it is the Path which God hath laid out for all that are in heaven and on earth.[114]   The Báb

Did the Báb and Bahá'u'lláh know each other? Only on a spiritual level. Bahá'u'lláh was a devoted follower of the Báb, who endangered His own life and suffered torture to promote the Báb's Message.

The twin Redeemers never met, yet their love for each other was boundless, to the extent that each was willing to die for the other. Only God can create such an intimate bond between two seeming strangers. The spiritual connection between the Báb and Bahá'u'lláh, their total awareness of one another without physical means, and their absolute devotion to each other present further evidence of their divine origin. In the history of humankind, we can find such an intimate and spiritual connection only between John the Baptist and Jesus.

The Báb and Bahá'u'lláh manifest a single Spirit. The oneness refers to the heavenly light, and not to the human mirror, which reflects the light:

> Indeed He [Bahá'u'lláh] is I and I am He.[115]
>
> The Báb

In spite of His supreme station, the Báb expressed absolute humility towards Bahá'u'lláh. No one has ever praised and glorified another as much as the Báb praised and glorified Bahá'u'lláh:

> Indeed any man whose eye gazeth upon His Words with true faith well deserveth Paradise; and one whose conscience beareth witness unto His Words with true faith shall abide in Paradise and attain the presence of God; and one whose tongue giveth utterance to His Words with true faith shall have his abode in Paradise, wherein he will be seized with ecstasy in praise and glorification of God, the Ever-Abiding.[116]   The Báb

Similarly the Báb expressed His lowliness before God:

> Verily no God is there but God; His is the kingdom of heaven and earth...and He [the Báb] Who speaketh at the bidding of His Lord is but the First to worship Him.[117]   The Báb

How do great Messengers relate to each other and to God? In two ways or on two levels: the station of separation and the station of oneness. Consider every one of God's Messengers as a brilliant light bulb in an exquisite chandelier. Each bulb radiates separately, and yet is connected with every other bulb through the light it radiates and through the one electrical system from which it draws power. Similarly, each Messenger relates to God and to every other Messenger in two ways: In one way, He remains a separate Being; in another, He is one with God and every other Messenger. Here Christ speaks in the state or station of oneness:

> My Father and I are one.   Christ (John 10:30)

> He who has seen me, has seen the Father.
>   Christ (John 14:9)

And here He speaks in the state or station of separation:

> My Father is greater than I.   Christ (John 14:29)

> Why do you call Me good? No one is good but One, that is, God.   Christ (Matt. 19:17)

In the following verses, first the lighted bulb (the Báb) speaks as "Me," then the source of the light in the bulb (God) speaks as "I:"

> The Lord hath, in truth, inspired Me: Verily, verily, I am God, He besides Whom there is none other God, and I am indeed the Ancient of Days.[118]   The Báb

Bahá'u'lláh also refers to the two stations:

> When I contemplate, O My God, the relationship that bindeth me to Thee, I am moved to proclaim to all created things, "Verily, I am God!"; and when I consider my own self, lo, I find it coarser than clay![119]   Bahá'u'lláh

The Báb declares that "by the leave of God," He conversed with Moses "from the midst of the Burning Bush:"

> Indeed We conversed with Moses by the leave of God from the midst of the Burning Bush in the Sinai and revealed an infinitesimal glimmer of Thy Light upon the Mystic Mount and its dwellers.[120]
>
> The Báb

He claims to speak only the Word of God and to abide only by His Will as did Jesus:

> We have in truth sent Thee forth unto all men, by the leave of God, invested with Our signs and reinforced by Our unsurpassed sovereignty. He is indeed the appointed Bearer of the Trust of God.[121]
>
> The Báb

> I have appointed Thee to be the Beginning and the End, the Seen and the Hidden. Verily We are the All-Knowing.[122]   The Báb

How Do Bahá'ís Intend to Unify the Diverse Religions of the World?

To love the world is to me no chore;
My trouble is the man next door.

God has a progressive plan for our planet. According to a Christian author:

> There is a unique harmony in the Bible. In Genesis the earth is created; in Revelation it passes away. In Genesis the sun and moon appear; in Revelation

there is no need for the sun or moon. In Genesis there is a garden; the home of man; in Revelation there is a city, the home of the nations. In Genesis we are introduced to Satan; in Revelation we see his doom. In Genesis we hear the first sob and see the first tear; in Revelation we read: "God shall wipe away all tears from their eyes; and there shall be no more death, neither sorrow, nor crying." In Genesis the curse is pronounced; in Revelation we read "There shall be no more curse." In Genesis we see our first parents driven from the tree of life; in Revelation welcomed back.[123]

Global unity is part of God's progressive plan for our time:

Then I myself will come to gather all nations and races and they shall come and see My glory [the glory of God]. *Isaiah 66:18*

The ultimate goal of Bahá'u'lláh's teachings is to create a unified world society, a global civilization in which everyone will see himself or herself as a unique cell in the body of humanity, working in perfect harmony with everyone else.

Bend your minds and wills to the education of the peoples and kindreds of the earth, that haply the dissensions that divide it may...be blotted out from its face, and all mankind become the upholders of one Order, and the inhabitants of one City...Ye dwell in one world, and have been created through the operation of one Will. Blessed is he who mingleth with all men in a spirit of utmost kindliness and love.[124] *Bahá'u'lláh*

The purpose of religion is to inspire love, tolerance, and hope—not hatred and prejudice. Yet untold millions have been killed and persecuted in the name of God.

A famous poet tells a story about three travelers who spoke different languages. During their journey they found a coin. Since they could not divide it, they decided to buy some food, and then to divide the food. Their inability to communicate led to a heated argument. At that point a fourth person, who spoke all three languages, came to their aid. When he learned about their argument, he smiled and said, "You all want the same fruit: namely, grapes." Bahá'u'lláh is the One who speaks to all faiths in a language they understand. In the Bahá'í teachings, the followers of all faiths can find fulfillment of their highest hopes and desires.

People worship the same God and ask Him for the same blessings. They want happiness, contentment, security, comfort, and peace. Despite common goals, they remain divided. They will only heed the Voice that speaks with the same authority as their own Teacher and Redeemer. Bahá'u'lláh speaks with that Voice.

In this age, Bahá'u'lláh has confirmed the divine origin of all great religions and the oneness of all Messengers and Prophets of God:

> Know thou assuredly that the essence of all the Prophets of God is one and the same. Their unity is absolute. God, the Creator, saith: There is no distinction whatsoever among the Bearers of My Message. They all have but one purpose; their

secret is the same secret. To prefer one in honor to another, to exalt certain ones above the rest, is in no wise to be permitted. Every true Prophet hath regarded His Message as fundamentally the same as the Revelation of every other Prophet gone before Him.[125]

Only the setting and dawning points of the sun change, not the sun itself. The same Spirit, the same Word, which the Báb calls "the Primal Will," appears in all great Messengers and Redeemers:

> And know thou that He indeed resembleth the sun. Were the risings of the sun to continue till the end that hath no end, yet there hath not been nor ever will be more than one sun; and were its settings to endure for evermore, still there hath not been nor ever will be more than one sun. It is this Primal Will which appeareth resplendent in every Prophet and speaketh forth in every revealed Book.[126]   The Báb

God is one and indivisible:

> I am...the First and the Last, the Beginning and the End.   Christ (Rev. 21:6)

Ponder the following verses. They declare that there never has been nor will ever be any Prophet other than the Báb:

> I [the divine Spirit] have appointed Thee to be the Beginning and the End, the Seen and the Hidden. Verily We are the All-Knowing. No one hath been or will ever be invested with prophethood other than Thee, nor hath any sacred Book been or will be revealed unto any one except Thee![127] The Báb

In our solar system, has there ever been or will there ever be a sun other than the sun? This principle is so powerful, it eliminates every trace of prejudice, separation, and superiority.

The following verses show that God Himself is the Savior. Since there is only *one* God, all those who speak for Him must also be *one*:

> For I am your Lord, your God, the Holy One of Israel, your Savior...I, even I, am the Lord, and apart from me there is no savior.   Isaiah 43:3,11

> There is no God apart from me, a righteous God and a Savior; there is none but me. Turn to me and be saved, all you ends of the earth.
> Isaiah 45:21-22

Because of their belief in the oneness of religion and the progressive revelation of truth, Bahá'ís can communicate with the followers of all great religions. In general, the followers of each of the world's great religions accept only their own Messenger and the ones who came before Him but deny the rest. For instance, Jews accept only three Messengers—Noah, Abraham, and Moses—but deny the rest. Christians accept only four Messengers—Noah, Abraham, Moses, and Jesus—but deny all the rest. Even the ones they accept, they do not consider equal with Jesus. Bahá'ís revere, in a spirit of oneness, all great Messengers and Teachers of the past: Noah, Abraham, Moses, Jesus, Muhammad, the Báb, and Bahá'u'lláh. They also recognize Buddha, Zoroaster, and Krishna, who are denied by Jews, Christians, and Muslims.

Bahá'u'lláh's message of oneness has unified millions from every religion, race, creed, and culture. The new Faith is a laboratory in which the unity of religion has been tested and tried with phenomenal success. It blends the peoples of our planet like threads of light into a tapestry of the utmost beauty and splendor.

Bahá'u'lláh teaches that all religions of God have the same purpose; they differ in name only. Behind the drifting clouds of differences lies a single source of light. A viewer can wear dark glasses to conceal the sun or colored glasses to see it in any colors she wants. She can also set many borders on the earth. But none of them can change this simple truth: There is one sun, one light, and one earth.

Behind the suffocating fumes of ideological conflicts and countless theological positions lies this simple truth: There is only one God, one humanity, and one faith. Divisiveness among religions and peoples has always been fueled by theological conflicts. "An elderly lady had heard a certain distinguished guest addressed as doctor. She found her way to his side and asked shyly, 'Doctor, may I ask you a question?' 'Certainly,' he said. 'Lately,' she said, 'I have been having a funny pain in my side...' The guest interrupted uncomfortably and said, 'I'm terribly sorry, madam, but the truth is, I'm a doctor of theology!' 'Oh,' she said with disappointment, 'I'm sorry!' She turned away, but then, overcome with curiosity, she turned back. 'Just one more question, doctor. Tell me, what kind of disease is theology?'"

People have been taught to believe that their religion is the only true religion, the only way to the Kingdom of Heaven. And they have tended to accept this belief as an unquestionable fact. As long as they do not examine other religions with an open mind, they can persist in their beliefs. But what happens when they step beyond the boundaries of tradition? They begin to notice an astonishing similarity between the fundamental teachings of all the great religions. Once they see this, they experience a "paradigm shift," and they find it hard to go back to their original beliefs. They are like the man who is told his hometown is the best; he can believe it as long as he does not venture into other towns.

In his classic work *The Structure of Scientific Revolution*, Thomas Kuhn "shows how almost every significant breakthrough in the field of scientific endeavor is first a break with tradition, with old ways of thinking, with old paradigms."[128]

An old man picked up a little girl and put her on his lap. The girl looked at the man's wrinkled face and asked, "Did God make you?" "Yes," said the old man. "Did God make me also?" "Yes," said the old man again. "Well," said the little girl, "don't you think that He is doing a better job now than He used to?" That is how the followers of each of the great faiths judge the ones sent before them. They think their faith is better or more true. This notion of superiority leads to prejudice, suspicion, and separation. Bahá'ís believe that all great faiths have come from God. The only difference between them is in renewal, relevance, and timing.

In a talk given in the United States in 1912, 'Abdu'l-Bahá said:

> The divine religion is reality, and reality is not multiple; it is one. Therefore, the foundations of the religious systems are one because all proceed from the indivisible reality; but the followers of these systems have disagreed; discord, strife and warfare have arisen among them, for they have forsaken the foundation and held to that which is but imitation and semblance. Inasmuch as imitations differ, enmity and dissension have resulted. For example, Jesus Christ—may my spirit be a sacrifice unto Him!—laid the foundation of eternal reality, but after His departure many sects and divisions appeared in Christianity. What was the cause of this? There is no doubt that they originated in dogmatic imitations, for the foundations of Christ were reality itself, in which no divergence exists. When imitations appeared, sects and denominations were formed.

> If Christians of all denominations and divisions should investigate reality, the foundations of Christ will unite them. No enmity or hatred will remain, for they will all be under the one guidance of reality itself. Likewise, in the wider field if all the existing religious systems will turn away from ancestral imitations and investigate reality, seeking the real meanings of the Holy Books, they will unite and agree upon the same foundation, reality itself. As long as they follow counterfeit doctrines or imitations instead of reality, animosity and discord will exist and increase.[129]

The Bahá'í Faith creates a new awareness and a new understanding of religion. Once people gain this awareness and insight, they exclaim, "It's so refreshing to learn about a faith that respects all faiths."

Although people believe in the uniqueness of their religion, somehow they sense that this belief does not fit into their understanding of a benevolent Creator who loves *all* His children. They hear a Voice in their soul murmuring, "The Creator cannot descend to a level lower than humans. He cannot care for *some* of His children, and ignore or abandon the rest."

In my youth I read various passages from the Qur'án from time to time. At one point I decided to read it from cover to cover. During this reading I was overtaken by a sense of awe and mystery. The feeling came from hearing the same Voice I had heard many times before, during repeated readings of the Bible. I can never forget that unearthly experience.

A student asked her professor, "Would it be possible for all the peoples of the world to live in America?" The professor paused, made some calculations, and said, "Yes, if they were all friends." The power of the Bahá'í Faith lies in this: It makes friends of old enemies.

The following diagram portrays the spiritual design for the "tabernacle of unity" as declared by Bahá'u'lláh.

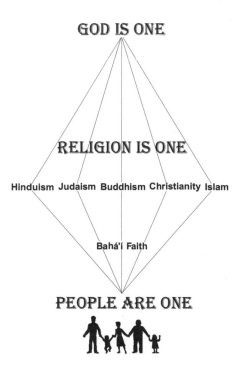

GOD IS ONE

RELIGION IS ONE

Hinduism Judaism Buddhism Christianity Islam

Bahá'í Faith

PEOPLE ARE ONE

On that day the Lord shall be one
Lord and his name the one name.
Zechariah 14:9

He Who is your Lord, the All Merciful,
cherisheth in His heart the desire of
beholding the entire human race
as one soul and one body.[130]
Bahá'u'lláh

In every dispensation, the light of Divine Guidance has been focused upon one central theme...In this wondrous Revelation, this glorious century, the foundation of the Faith of God, and the distinguishing feature of His Law, is the consciousness of the oneness of mankind.[131]   'Abdu'l-Bahá

This prophecy is specifically addressed to us; it is both an invitation and a warning to the people of our time:

Gather together, gather together...before the appointed time arrives...before the day of the Lord's wrath comes upon you. Seek the Lord, all you humble of the land, you who do what he commands. Seek righteousness, seek humility; perhaps you will be sheltered on the day of the Lord's anger.
Zephaniah 2:1-3

Thus, our failure to bring unity will lead to grave consequences for all humanity.

A president's fondest dream was to initiate "a thousand points of light" in his nation. Yet, despite his power, he failed. Bahá'u'lláh's purpose is to make every heart an immortal point of light. Every Bahá'í on this planet works for this very end.

Only God can touch hearts, only He can build "the house:"

Unless the Lord builds the house, its builders have toiled in vain.   Psalms 127:1

Prayers for unity from the Bahá'í Scriptures:

O my God! O my God! Unite the hearts of Thy servants, and reveal to them Thy great purpose. May they follow Thy commandments and abide in Thy law. Help them, O God, in their endeavor, and grant them strength to serve Thee. O God! Leave them not to themselves, but guide their steps by the light of Thy knowledge, and cheer their hearts by Thy love. Verily, Thou art their Helper and their Lord.[132]   Bahá'u'lláh

O Lord God! Make us as waves of the sea, as flowers of the garden, united, agreed through the bounties of Thy love. O Lord!...make all mankind as stars shining from the same height of glory, as perfect fruits growing upon Thy tree of life.

Verily, Thou art the Almighty, the Self-Subsistent, the Giver, the Forgiving, the Pardoner, the Omniscient, the One Creator.[133]   'Abdu'l-Bahá

Is World Peace a Dream or a Destiny?

We see the stirrings of a new dawn in human history. Throughout all ages, dictators have dominated the world. Recently we have seen them falling like autumn leaves. "After President Roosevelt offered a flowery toast to Premier Stalin as a lover of peace, the Soviets awaited a toast by Churchill. Churchill growled in a whisper, 'But Stalin does not want peace.' But at the urging of his staff, he rose and said, 'To Premier Stalin, whose conduct of foreign policy manifests a desire for peace.' Then, away from the translator, he muttered, 'A piece of Poland,

a piece of Czechoslovakia, a piece of Romania.'"
The age of those dictators is finally coming to an end.

The Bahá'í Faith teaches that world peace is inevitable, and that genuine peace can only come through world unity. If the various nations, religions, and races were unified, there would be no reason for war. But without unity, war or preparation for war will continue.

Had humanity responded fully and promptly to Bahá'u'lláh's plan for peace, the wars of the 20th Century—the most deadly in human history—would not have happened. Similarly, if the world awakens to the relevance and urgency of the Bahá'í teachings now, the forces that generate war will disappear. War is a symptom of a disease: The disease is disunity. As soon as Bahá'u'lláh's unifying remedy is applied, the disease will vanish.

> The well-being of mankind, its peace and security are unattainable unless and until its unity is firmly established...Soon will the present day Order be rolled up, and a new one spread out in its stead.[134]
>
> Bahá'u'lláh

A captain once invited three friends—a Jew, a Christian, and a Muslim—to his ship. While the three were sitting on the deck enjoying the scenery, a huge wave threw them into the sea. They panicked and began shouting and moving in different directions. The captain came quickly to their rescue. He grabbed the hair of the first one. But it came off; it was a wig. Then he got hold of the arm of the second one. But it came off; it too was artificial. Finally he reached for the leg of the third one. You guessed it, that too came off. The three were near drowning, and each of them was crying in desperation, "Save me, save me!" The captain shouted back, "I will, only if you stick together!" The human race can only survive if its members stick together.

The only thing the world has in common at this point in history is "isms:" sectarian-ism, race-ism, sex-ism, national-ism, and commun-ism. All these isms must change into one-ism.

Recognition of the oneness of the human race is the backbone of lasting peace. We live on a fragile spacecraft. Our survival depends on cooperation; we need each other. We need someone to sing and someone to hear; someone to complain and someone to listen; someone to cry and someone to wipe away the tears; someone to tell jokes and someone to laugh; and someone to get sick and someone to offer a cure. A doctor told a young patient that her tonsils had to be removed. The patient asked, "Will removing them damage my health?" "No, your tonsils serve no purpose" the doctor told her. "Why then did God give them to me?" asked the inquiring patient. "Well, I think He gave them to you so that I can afford my next vacation!"

We all have a responsibility to do our share to free the human race from the scourge of war. ***We should not underestimate our capacity to change the world***. What brings about the change, what generates love and peace and unity, is always God's Power. We need to empty ourselves and, like reeds, allow God's Voice to awaken and enchant us—and to echo that Voice until it is heard in every part of the world by every citizen of our planet. Let us pray that the powers we lay at the service of arms may be elevated to a higher purpose: creating hope, beauty, and happiness in our lives. Without this elevation, we will perish in despair.

Why Do Bahá'ís Emphasize "Independent Investigation of Truth"?

We all face two alternatives: Either we choose our beliefs or chance will choose them for us. "There is a time when we must firmly choose the course we will follow, or the relentless drift of events will make the decision for us."

In a talk delivered in the United States in 1912, 'Abdu'l-Bahá said:

Behold how the sun shines upon all creation, but only surfaces that are pure and polished can reflect its glory and light...it behooves us all to be lovers of truth. Let us seek her in every season and in every country, being careful never to attach ourselves to personalities. Let us see the light wherever it shines...If five people meet together to seek for truth, they must begin by cutting themselves free from all their own special conditions and renouncing all perceived ideas. In order to find truth we must give up our prejudices, our own small trivial notions; an open receptive mind is essential. If our chalice is full of self, there is no room in it for the water of life. The fact that we imagine ourselves to be right and everybody else wrong is the greatest of all obstacles in the path towards unity, and unity is necessary if we would reach truth, for truth is one.[135]

The source and the essence of all virtues is love for knowledge and truth:

> The essence of all that We have revealed for thee is Justice, is for man to free himself from idle fancy and imitation, discern with the eye of oneness His glorious handiwork, and look into all things with a searching eye.[136] Bahá'u'lláh

Love for knowledge and truth can only be attained through an unbiased and impartial search. To study the principle of independent investigation, we need to do some soul-searching. And a good way is to begin with this question: What would be my religion if I were raised in

- a Hindu family?   • a Christian family?
- a Jewish family?   • a Muslim family?
- a Buddhist family?   • an atheist family?

Most people admit that their religion would consist of whatever their parents taught them. What does this suggest? That most people are satisfied with, and regard as truth, what their ancestors believed and practiced. One's religion is thus determined by chance and often accepted without investigation. How many people do you know who have impartially investigated even one of the world's great religions? And how many people do you know who are following a religion other than the one followed by their parents? To the conformist and closed-minded Jews of His day, Jesus said:

> I am telling you what I have seen in **the Father's**
> presence, and you do what you have heard from
> **your** father.   John 8:38

Should we be "Moonies" if our ancestors worshipped
the moon, and "Sunnies" if they worshipped the
sun, and "Stonies" if they worshipped stones?
"Some people are like an anchor that lies always
in the sea yet never learns to swim."

> Joe: What do you believe about God?
> Moe: I believe what my church believes.
> Joe: What does your church believe?
> Moe: My church believes what I believe.
> Joe: What do you and your church believe?
> Moe: We both believe the same thing.

Psychologist Dr. Robert Anthony explains how our
beliefs affect our behavior:

> Once a person believes that something is true,
> whether or not it is, he then acts as if it were. He
> will instinctively seek to collect facts to support
> the belief no matter how false it may be. No one
> will be able to convince him otherwise unless,
> through personal experience or study, he is ready
> to change. Hence, it is easy to see that, if one
> accepts something which is not true, all subse-
> quent actions and reactions will be based upon a
> false belief...

> The average person never comes near reaching
> his unlimited potential because he is living under
> the false assumption that he already knows the
> truth. He believes what his parents told him, what
> his teachers have taught him, what he has read,

and what his religion preaches without actually proving anything for himself.[137]

Bahá'u'lláh teaches that religion is too important to be left to chance and imitation, that every individual should examine other religions and other ways of life, and then choose. Some people refuse to take even one step out of their comfort zone for fear of losing what they have. "An old man was standing on a crowded bus. A young man standing next to him asked, 'What time is it?' The old man refused to reply. The young man moved on. The old man's friend, sensing something wrong, asked, 'Why were you so discourteous to the young man asking for the time?' The old man answered, 'If I had given him the time of day, next he would want to know where I am going. Then we might talk about our interests. If we did that, he might invite himself to my house for dinner. If he did that he would meet my lovely daughter. If he met her, they would fall in love. I don't want my daughter to marry someone who can't afford a watch.'" Fear of the unknown and attachment to one's own beliefs stifle curiosity and the courage to seek new spiritual horizons.

Did you hear about a man who invented a device for looking through a wall? Do you know what he called it? A window. Every soul needs a window to look out and to let light in.

No loss can come from seeking, from gaining knowledge and awareness. In fact, just the opposite is true: ***Every good comes from seeking, and every evil from not seeking, from closing the mind***.

True opinions can prevail only if the facts to which they refer are known; if they are not known, false ideas are just as effective as true ones, if not a little more effective.

Throughout history religious leaders have discouraged their followers from investigating other faiths. This enlightening statement from a Christian publication is an exception; it shows a radical change of perspective:

Have you ever thought or said, "I have my own religion. It is a very personal matter. I do not discuss it with others"? True, religion is very personal—virtually from birth religious or ethical ideas are implanted in our mind by our parents and relatives. As a consequence, we usually follow the religious ideals of our parents and grandparents. Religion has become almost a matter of family tradition. What is the result of that process? In many cases others have chosen our religion for us. It has simply been a matter of where we were born and when. Or, as historian Arnold Toynbee indicated, an individual's adherence to a certain faith is often determined by "the geographical accident of the locality of his birth-place."

Is it reasonable to assume that the religion imposed at one's birth is necessarily the whole truth? If you were born in Italy or South America, then, without any choice, you were probably raised a Catholic. If you were born in India, then likely you automatically became a Hindu or, if from the Punjab, perhaps a Sikh. If your parents were from Pakistan, then you would obviously be a Muslim.

And if you were born in a Socialist country over the last few decades, you might have had no choice but to be raised an atheist.

Therefore, is the religion of one's birth automatically the true one, approved by God? If that had been the concept followed over the millenniums, many among mankind would still be practicing primitive shamanism and ancient fertility cults, on the premise that "what was good enough for my ancestors is good enough for me."

With the wide diversity of religious expression that has developed around the world over the past 6,000 years, it is at least educational and mind broadening to understand what others believe and how their beliefs originated. And it might also open up vistas of a more concrete hope for your future.[138]

Consider also the following statement from a Muslim author and scholar:

We are proud of ourselves because we know more about science and technology than our parents and ancestors. We readily accept what is better and more advanced than what our parents have had. Yet, many of us do not hesitate to follow our parents blindly in religion, even if it means doing something we do not fully believe in.[139]

By far the most important freedom is spiritual freedom. Every consequence is temporary except the spiritual, yet many ignore this God-given right. As psychologist Wayne Dyer notes:

We can respect and even appreciate the past and the ways of our ancestors. We can love them for having chosen to go their own way. But to be attached to having to live and think the way others before you did, because you showed up looking like them in form, is to deny yourself enlightenment. This is how people and their institutions have controlled others for thousands of years.[140]

Take a look at all of the people who are fighting in wars around the globe today, and you see them suffering and dying in the name of tradition. They are taught that what their ancestors believed is what they must believe. With this logic they perpetuate the suffering in their own lives and in the lives of their assigned enemies.[141]

As a human being you were built to think for yourself. Your mind is going to rebel with anxiety ...if you don't allow yourself the freedom to think up to your full...capacity.[142]

The laity are following their leaders; the leaders are following the laity. A French revolutionary once said, "There go my people and I must find out where they go, so I can lead them."

Unquestioned conformity is perhaps the most common cause of ignorance. Most people follow the phantoms of their own culture. They walk in the ways of their own ancient ancestors. They choose their robes but not their religion; their fish but not their faith; their doctor but not their destiny. Whatever chance hands them, they accept. Whatever their culture gives them, they worship. Whatever their family tells them, they follow.

Christ repeatedly asked Christians to investigate the news of His coming. As demonstrated in the books

I Shall Come Again, and *The Glory of the Father*, He often used the word "Watch!" in place of "Investigate!"

> What I say to you, I say to everyone: "Watch!"
> Mark 13:37

> Be always on the watch...that you may be able to stand before the Son of Man.   Luke 21:36

We must empty ourselves before we can be filled. We must leave all our preconceived notions behind. "The humble are the empty vessels God loves to fill."

> The fact that we imagine ourselves to be right and everybody else wrong is the greatest of all obstacles in the path towards unity...[143]
> 'Abdu'l-Bahá

Knowledge is light; ignorance is darkness. When we stand in the dark we experience fear and anxiety, we imagine danger. As soon as light comes, our fear vanishes. Truth is light; it extends our vision and makes us free. Why then are so many afraid of the light? Why are so many afraid to investigate? "The secret of happiness is freedom, and the secret of freedom is courage."

Knowledge of our spiritual destiny sheds light on our path even unto eternity. In life it manifests an enduring purpose, and in death it reveals the glimmering of eternal life. It takes away all fears.

> Give me the liberty to know, to think, to believe, and to utter freely, according to conscience, above all liberties.

Freedom of choice is one of God's most magnificent gifts. The consequences of the choices we make are enormous; we must make them with the utmost care:

> See, I am setting before you today a blessing and a curse—the blessing if you obey the commands of the Lord...the curse if you disobey the commands.   Deuteronomy 11:26-27

On the journey towards God, no one can blame others for his or her failure. No one can say, "My parents prevented me" or "My pastor misled me." God leaves the door open to all, and declares that He will accept no excuses from anyone:

> See, I have placed before you an open door that no one can shut.   Christ (Rev. 3:8)

Truth unifies; falsehood divides. If we seek the truth with impartial and open minds, we will all discover the three unifying onenesses that are the essence and purpose of this book: *one God, one faith, one people*. Acknowledging these three onenesses will create a power that will transform our planet and its peoples. What prevents us from seeing this truth is the veil of false assumptions, fantasies, and illusions.

We all have our own share of illusions and false assumptions. The difference is how many, and how attached we are to them. The incredible power of illusions comes from this: They hide from the one who holds them! We are quick to see other people's illusions, but not our own. Just as we get used to our own odors, we get used to our fantasies. As much truth is visible as we have minds to know and hearts to see.

Do Bahá'ís Have Clergy?

In the Bahá'í Faith there is no clergy. Tradition has taught the faithful followers of nearly all religions to leave significant spiritual decisions to religious leaders. Even in their relationship with God, some people look to priests as mediators for forgiveness. This long history of dependency has diminished people's curiosity and self-trust. The time has come for believers everywhere to become independent seekers, learners, and lovers of truth.

The Bahá'í community is directed by a unique democratic method based on spiritual principles such as purity of motives and love for justice and truth rather than personal concerns and interests. The functions of the clergy are carried out not only by individual Bahá'ís, but also by elected assemblies on the local and national levels. The Universal House of Justice, also an elected body, coordinates and directs the Bahá'í community on the international level.

> In administering the affairs of the community, the institutions of the Bahá'í Faith practice a form of consultation that involves full and frank discussion of issues. Matters are discussed with a desire to find the facts and to come to a decision based on spiritual principles, unhampered by personal attachment to points of view. The Bahá'í scriptures state: "The shining spark of truth comes forth only after the clash of differing opinions." While the goal of consultation is unanimous agreement, when unanimity cannot be reached, the majority prevails.[144]

Wisdom is the greatest virtue. But how can we attain wisdom? The easiest and most practical way is to seek the views of others, to learn from the experiences of competent and impartial people.

> Say: no man can attain his true station except through his justice. No power can exist except through unity. No welfare and no well-being can be attained except through consultation.[146]
>
> Bahá'u'lláh

> Man must consult in all things, for this will lead him to the depths of each problem and enable him to find the right solution.[145]   'Abdu'l-Bahá

Those who have knowledge and wisdom should not feel superior to others. The path of knowing and loving God is paved with forbearance, love, good-will, and humility; not with pride and self-glory:

> Show forbearance and benevolence and love to one another. Should any one among you be incapable of grasping a certain truth, or be striving to comprehend it, show forth, when conversing with him, a spirit of extreme kindliness and good-will. Help him to see and recognize the truth, without esteeming yourself to be, in the least, superior to him, or to be possessed of greater endowments.[147]   Bahá'u'lláh

Prophecies declare that "at the end of the age" everything will be made new. The Bahá'í social order is so new, it cannot be compared with any other order. Its success in fostering and protecting the unity and harmony of the Bahá'í community and moving it forward towards a glorious fulfillment, through the noblest means, presents evidence of its distinction and divine origin. The present Bahá'í community, which encompasses 120,000 centers, 17,000 local assemblies, and 175 national assemblies in over 200 countries and territories, offers a perfect model for the future world order, when all humanity acknowledges Bahá'u'lláh's Revelation.

Bahá'u'lláh's New World Order, unparalleled in all history, offers one more evidence of His divine origin. As Machiavelli wrote, "It must be remembered that there is nothing more difficult to plan, more uncertain of success, nor more dangerous to manage, than the creation of a new order of things."

How Do the Great Religions Differ?

Teaching should always be adapted to the learner. Christ spoke to simple people living in a simple world. Since His time the world has grown steadily more complex. What worked then may not work now.

Just as different individuals have different needs, so do the peoples of each age. "The minister was telling the congregation that God knows what is best for us. We are like flowers. 'You know roses grow best in sunlight, but fuchsias require shade to grow,' he said. A woman came up to him afterward bubbling over with praise. 'Pastor, that was just a wonderful sermon. I never could figure out just what was wrong with my fuchsias!'"

As a child needs new guidance at each stage of development, so does the human race. God has a plan and purpose for us, which He reveals progressively, through His Messengers, according to our needs and maturity. The Bahá'í Faith is the latest—but not the final—expression of that divine plan and purpose.

In Bahá'u'lláh's teachings, the spiritual knowledge brought by God's past Messengers has been expanded and adapted to our maturity. This is the difference between the Bahá'í Faith and the other great faiths.

> All created things have their degree or stage of maturity...Similarly there are periods and stages in the collective life of humanity. At one time it was passing through its stage of childhood, at another its period of youth, but now it has entered its long-predicted phase of maturity, the evidences of which are everywhere apparent...That which was applicable to human needs during the early history of the race can neither meet nor satisfy the demands of this day...The gifts and blessings of the period of youth, although timely and sufficient during the adolescence of mankind, are now incapable of meeting the requirements of its maturity.[148]
>
> 'Abdu'l-Bahá

> I gave you milk, not solid food, for you were not ready for it. Indeed, you are still not ready.
>
> I Corinthians 3:2

What happens if we continue to give a growing child nothing but milk? Starvation, stress, and disease will set in. That is what is happening to the spiritual life of the world. God has once again prepared a beautiful banquet with the most nourishing foods. In His supreme love, He invites everyone to come and enjoy the blessings and bounties beyond anything they have ever seen:

No eye has seen, no ear has heard, no mind has conceived what God has prepared for those who love him...   I Corinthians 2:9

But many are ignoring the invitation. They present all kinds of reasons to excuse themselves. Some of them don't like the name of the Host, others don't like the door to the banquet; some don't like the invitation card, others don't like the menu; some say they have their own special banquet, others are too busy, and still others are too attached to their bottles! They are quite patient; they have waited for 2,000 or 3,000 years; they can wait another 1,000.

God is the supreme teacher. He does not delay His help for even an instant. The evidence around us points to a dire need for a helping hand.

The face of the world hath altered. The way of God and the religion of God have ceased to be of any worth in the eyes of men.[149]   Bahá'u'lláh

Who else except God and what else except religion can restore love, hope, and peace to the heart of the world?

Religion is, verily, the chief instrument for the establishment of order in the world, and of tranquillity amongst its peoples...The greater the decline of religion, the more grievous the way-wardness of the ungodly. This cannot but lead in the end to chaos and confusion.[150]   Bahá'u'lláh

As the body of man needeth a garment to clothe it, so the body of mankind must needs be adorned with the mantle of justice and wisdom. Its robe is the Revelation vouchsafed unto it by God.[151]   Bahá'u'lláh

Each of the world's great religions represents a chapter in the book of divine knowledge entrusted to humanity. As we advance, God adds, once in about every thousand years, a new chapter to the book. The new chapter reiterates and expands some of the fundamentals found in the previous ones, such as loving God and being kind, honest, and charitable. These virtues never change. They stand as eternal and unchanging as God Himself.

Each new chapter also introduces some *new* instructions and information, such as those found in the Bahá'í Scriptures about unifying the human race and creating a new social order. Religions differ only in relation to social teachings, not in the fundamental spiritual truths. Forgiveness, faith, self-control, self-respect, self-sacrifice, sincerity, justice, detachment, and love—these virtues have been, and always will be, the very life and light of the world. Thus the only difference between the Bahá'í Faith and other faiths is in social, not spiritual, teachings. By studying each of the succeeding chapters of the book of divine knowledge, we gain a deeper understanding of previous ones. We also grow in faith, for we recognize the oneness, the infinite wisdom, and the greatness of its supreme Author and Designer.

This progressive revelation of truth and knowledge will continue forever:

> Indeed no religion shall We ever inaugurate unless it be renewed in the days to come. This is a promise We solemnly have made. Verily We are supreme over all things...[152]   The Báb

What Is Bahá'u'lláh's Plan for a Peaceful and Prosperous World?

We cannot build a new, peaceful, and prosperous world with obstacles like ignorance, inequality, apathy, selfishness, poverty, prejudice, and a lack of communication. The following are some of the principles Bahá'u'lláh presented for building a new world order:

- *Universal and compulsory education.* True education is the key to the prevention of all human suffering. True education not only enriches the mind but molds the character as well. It fosters the development of all human potential—physical, mental, emotional, social, moral, and spiritual. Every child must learn to practice justice, love, and wisdom. Learning to read and write, and master science, literature, and technology are only a small part of the total education a child must receive.

  The primary, the most urgent requirement is the promotion of education. It is inconceivable that any nation should achieve prosperity and success unless this paramount, this fundamental concern is carried forward. The principal reason for the decline and fall of peoples is ignorance. Today the masses of the people are uninformed even as to ordinary affairs, how much less do they grasp the core of the important problems and complex needs of the time.[153]   'Abdu'l-Bahá

• *Equality of men and women*. Each gender has special talents and can make special contributions to society. Women have had fewer opportunities for developing their talents. Their profound influence on children makes them especially deserving of new and greater opportunities for spiritual growth and self-enhancement.

> Women and men have been and will always be equal in the sight of God...The most beloved of people before God are the most steadfast and those who have surpassed others in their love for God, exalted be His glory...[154]
>
> Bahá'u'lláh

> Humanity is like a bird with its two wings— the one is male, the other female. Unless both wings are strong and impelled by some common force, the bird cannot fly heavenwards. According to the spirit of this age, women must advance and fulfill their mission in all departments of life, becoming equal to men. They must be on the same level as men and enjoy equal rights. This is my earnest prayer and it is one of the fundamental principles of Bahá'u'lláh.[155]   'Abdu'l-Bahá

• *Elimination of poverty*. There should be a fair distribution of wealth. The Bahá'í Faith has laws and teachings that make this possible.

> **O YE RICH ONES ON EARTH!**
> The poor in your midst are My trust; guard ye My trust, and be not intent only on your own ease.[156]   Bahá'u'lláh

O CHILDREN OF DUST!
Tell the rich of the midnight sighing of the poor, lest heedlessness lead them into the path of destruction, and deprive them of the Tree of Wealth. To give and to be generous are attributes of Mine; well is it with him that adorneth himself with My virtues.[157]

Bahá'u'lláh

It is important to limit riches, as it is also of importance to limit poverty. Either extreme is not good...When we see poverty allowed to reach a condition of starvation, it is a sure sign that somewhere we shall find tyranny... There must be special laws made, dealing with these extremes of riches and want...The government of the countries should conform to the Divine Law which gives equal justice to all.[158]

'Abdu'l-Bahá

• *Work is not a curse or a burden, but a blessing and a gift from God*. Many people do not enjoy their work. "If you haven't made up your mind about reincarnation, just watch the way some people come back to life at quitting time."

The hand that is rough with labor is fit to hold the hand of God. In the estimation of God, Bahá'u'lláh teaches, work equates with worship. All are encouraged to invest their talents in a craft or profession.

It is enjoined upon every one of you to engage in some form of occupation...We have graciously exalted your engagement in such work to the rank of worship unto God, the

True One. Ponder ye in your hearts the grace
and the blessings of God and render thanks
unto Him at eventide and at dawn. Waste not
your time in idleness and sloth. Occupy yourselves with that which profiteth yourselves
and others.[159]   Bahá'u'lláh

Bahá'u'lláh's teachings change the pain of working into the pleasure of serving and glorifying
God. They transform a worker's perspective from
"how many hours did I put in" into "how much
did I put in the hours." A cheerful attitude always
lightens the burden. The worthiest gifts to God
are wrapped in a desire to serve Him and tied
with a passion to love Him. Bahá'u'lláh teaches
that serving and pleasing people is the same as
serving and pleasing God.

• *Elimination of prejudice.* Being prejudiced is
identical to being narrow-minded. A mind that
is already set stands as an obstacle to understanding, harmony, peace, and unity. Today, many
kinds of prejudice prevail: racism, sexism, sec-
tarianism, and nationalism.

Ye observe how the world is divided against
itself, how many a land is red with blood...
And the breeding-ground of all these tragedies
is prejudice: prejudice of race and nation, of
religion, of political opinion; and the root
cause of prejudice is blind imitation of the
past—imitation in religion, in racial attitudes,
in national bias, in politics. So long as this
aping of the past pesisteth, just so long will
the foundations of the social order be blown

to the four winds, just so long will humanity be continually exposed to direst peril.[160]

'Abdu'l-Bahá

• *Unity in diversity.* We have many distinct walls. Let us make a bridge to connect them all. "The world is slowly learning that because two believers think differently, neither need be wicked." Unity in diversity declares this most fundamental message:

> *In essentials—unity*
> *In nonessentials—diversity*
> *In all things—love*

'Abdu'l-Bahá explains this principle:

When divers shades of thought, temperament and character, are brought together under the power and influence of one central agency, the beauty and glory of human perfection will be revealed and made manifest. Naught but the celestial potency of the Word of God, which ruleth and transcendeth the realities of all things, is capable of harmonizing the divergent thoughts, sentiments, ideas, and convictions of the children of men.[161]

'Abdu'l-Bahá

• *A new world order*. A religion that intends to unify the world must have a plan for global unity and set an example of order and harmony in the way it directs its own affairs.

Soon will the present-day order be rolled up, and a new one spread out in its stead. Verily, thy Lord speaketh the truth, and is the Knower of things unseen.[162] Bahá'u'lláh

The day is approaching when We will have rolled up the world and all that is therein, and spread out a new order in its stead. He, verily, is powerful over all things.[163]

Bahá'u'lláh

Bend your minds and wills to the education of the peoples and kindreds of the earth, that haply the dissensions that divide it may...be blotted out from its face, and all mankind become the upholders of one Order, and the inhabitants of one City.[164]   Bahá'u'lláh

Shoghi Effendi, the Guardian of the Bahá'í Faith, provided an outline of Bahá'u'lláh's New World Order:

The unity of the human race, as envisaged by Bahá'u'lláh, implies the establishment of a world commonwealth in which all nations, races, creeds, and classes are closely and permanently united, and in which the autonomy of its state members and the personal freedom and initiative of the individuals that compose them are definitely and completely safeguarded. This commonwealth must, as far as we can visualize it, consist of a world legislature...A world executive, backed by an international Force, will carry out the decisions arrived at, and apply the laws enacted by, this world legislature...A world tribunal will...deliver its compulsory and final verdict in all and any disputes that may arise between the various elements constituting this universal system. A mechanism of world inter-communication will be devised, embracing the whole planet...A world metropolis will act as the nerve center of a world civilization...The economic resources of the world will be organized, its sources of raw materials will be tapped and fully utilized, its markets will be coordinated and developed, and the distribution of its products will be equitably regulated.[165]

This is the plan prepared for the whole earth, this is the hand stretched out over all the nations. For the Lord of Hosts has prepared his plan: who shall frustrate it? His is the hand stretched out, and who shall turn it back?   Isaiah 14:26-27

• *A **universal auxiliary language***. According to one source, the people of our planet speak 6,000 languages and dialects. As the world shrinks, communication between its inhabitants becomes more critical. A universal auxiliary language is an essential medium for fostering fellowship and understanding among nations.

We have enjoined upon the Trustees of the House of Justice either to choose one language from among those now existing or to adopt a new one, and in like manner to select a common script, both of which should be taught in all the schools of the world. Thus will the earth be regarded as one country and one home. The most glorious fruit of the tree of knowledge is this exalted word: Of one tree are all ye the fruit, and of one bough the leaves. Let not man glory in this that he loveth his country, let him rather glory in this that he loveth his kind.[166]   Bahá'u'lláh

Lack of communication not only breaks down marriages but also nations.

People don't get along because they fear each other. People fear each other because they don't know each other. They don't know each other because they have not properly communicated with each other.

Martin Luther King

In a global language lies enormous powers:

And the Lord said, behold, they are one people, and they have all one language; and this is only the beginning of what they will do; and now nothing they have imagined they can do will be impossible to them.

Genesis 11:6

• *We are, in essence, spiritual beings*. Our souls depend on spiritual nourishment as much as our bodies on physical. Whether it is the cell or the soul, starvation eventually leads to death. Spirituality is the salt of the soul; without it, the soul spoils. It must be sprinkled on everyone, every day. "A 5-year-old boy was watching his mother change the baby. When she overlooked sprinkling the tot's backside with talcum powder, the 5-year-old reminded her, 'Hey, Mom, you forgot to salt him!'"

...from the very beginning, the children must receive divine education and must continually be reminded to remember their God. Let the love of God pervade their inmost being, commingled with their mother's milk.[167]

'Abdu'l-Bahá

What Is Biological Prejudice?

Prejudice lies at the root of all evils. Eliminating it is one of Bahá'u'lláh's prime principles. Perhaps the lowest and worst of all prejudices is biological: the illusion that physical differences give us good reasons for feeling superior. If someone is proud of his or her humility, perhaps we can forgive that! But to be proud of one's gender or race, or of any other genetic feature, is to descend to a level lower than that of an insect. For various species of animals— whether hunters, like wolf, lion, and tiger; or peaceful, like panda, dove, and butterfly—never use color as a sign of supremacy and superiority.

Anyone who uses anything physical—race, gender, age, height, weight, beauty, or disability—as a means of establishing superiority or inferiority shows a lack of understanding of the true essence of being human. Most likely such an individual is seeking, however unconsciously, to conceal deficiencies of his or her own soul with veils and clouds of illusion.

Biological prejudice is the lowest and cheapest means of separation, superiority, and self-satisfaction. At the heart of it lies the very denial of God's justice. It implies that in creating His masterpiece— human beings—God either deliberately discriminated against some of them or suffered from lapses of judgment.

At the heart of it lies also the denial of the very essence of human beings: their souls. For it implies that the worth of a person lies not in spiritual splendors but in physical features. Finding one's superiority in one's color, gender, or any other physical feature communicates this message: My essence, my true honor, worth, and value lie not in my love and the light in my heart, but in my looks and the lightness of my skin; not in my soul and service to humankind, but in my gender; not in my character, but in my color.

Then what is prejudice? It is the descent of human beings from the highest and noblest plane of perfection to the lowest and cheapest. It is ignoring the light and adoring the lamp. It is demeaning the immortal gift, and glorifying and clinging to the disposable cover. It is degrading the station of the soul to the state of a cell. It is reducing the rank of an angel to the role of an ant. It is diminishing the splendors of the soul to the lowliness of the soil. It is debasing the lofty bird of heaven to the lowly bug of the earth. It is exchanging the glories and grandeur of God's image for the worth of a worm. For that is what our bodies will at last become!

In a letter sent to a pompous, worldly, and cruel king, Bahá'u'lláh asks this question: Can anyone tell the difference between the skeleton of a beggar and that of a prince? Let us ask a similar question: Can anyone tell the difference between the worms that have thrived on white skin or black skin? Fed on men's flesh or women's flesh?

An epitaph on a burial marker:

Here I lie by the chancel door,
Here I lie because I'm poor,
The farther in, the more you pay,
Here I lie as warm as they.

In *The Hidden Words*, Bahá'u'lláh uses the word *dust* nine times as a heading to show the worth of our physical form. He uses expressions such as: O Son of Dust, O Moving Form of Dust, O Offspring of Dust.

> Know ye not why We created you all from the same *dust*? That no one should exalt himself over the other. Ponder at all times in your hearts how ye were created. Since We have created you all from one same substance it is incumbent on you to be even as one soul...that from your inmost being, by your deeds and actions, the signs of oneness and the essence of detachment may be made manifest.[168] Bahá'u'lláh

> All will I gather beneath the one-colored covering of the *dust* and efface all these diverse colors save them that choose My own, and that is purging from every color.[169] Bahá'u'lláh

What Are the Bahá'í Teachings on Marriage and Family?

Our world suffers from a desperate sense of separation and a scarcity of love. The highest rates of murder and assault are found among friends and family members. Today, parents and children spend little time together. This prophecy from Micah describes the trends of our time:

> For a son dishonors his father, a daughter rises up against her mother, a daughter-in-law against her mother-in-law—a man's enemies are the members of his own household.   Micah 7:6

Bahá'u'lláh has declared the dawning of the age of peace and oneness between all members of the human race, including family members. He has come to turn the hearts of parents and children towards each other. This, too, has been prophesied:

> See, I will send you the prophet Elijah before that great and dreadful day of the Lord comes. He will turn the hearts of the fathers to their children, and the hearts of the children to their fathers.
>
> Malachi 4:5-6

A good family starts with a good marriage. Bahá'í teachings describe marriage as a divine institution, a fundamental feature of the design of creation. It will never be outmoded, for it reflects the very purpose for which God created the universe.

> The purpose of God in creating man hath been, and will ever be, to enable him to know his Creator and to attain His Presence.[170]   Bahá'u'lláh

Marriage is a sacred pledge not only between a man and a woman, but also between a couple and God. It is not a contract for convenience but a covenant between two lovers of God who decide to become one physically and spiritually. This awareness elevates marriage from the physical plane to the spiritual. According to Bahá'í principles, those united by the marriage bond should not base their relationship on convenience or personal needs and desires, but on the Will of God. An evidence of this is the Bahá'í marriage vow, which reads, "We will all, verily, abide by the Will of God." The spiritual bond formed on earth should endure for all eternity.

> Marriage, among the mass of the people, is a physical bond, and this union can only be temporary, since it is foredoomed to a physical separation at the close.

> Among the people of Bahá [Bahá'ís], however, marriage must be a union of the body and of the spirit as well...[171]
> 'Abdu'l-Bahá

In a letter addressed to two Bahá'ís who planned to get married, 'Abdu'l-Bahá wrote:

> O ye two believers in God! The Lord, peerless is He, hath made woman and man to abide with each other in the closest companionship, and to be even as a single soul. They are two helpmates, two intimate friends, who should be concerned about the welfare of each other.

> If they live thus, they will pass through this world with perfect contentment, bliss, and peace of heart, and become the object of divine grace and favor in the Kingdom of heaven. But if they do other than this, they will live out their lives in great bitterness, longing at every moment for death, and will be shamefaced in the heavenly realm.

> Strive, then, to abide, heart and soul, with each other as two doves in the nest, for this is to be blessed in both worlds.[172]

Love in Bahá'í marriage is not based simply on physical attraction but on attraction to God.

Real love is impossible unless one turns his face towards God and be attracted to His Beauty.[173]

'Abdu'l-Bahá

If we love people, including our family, for the sake of God and not for their assets, our love remains unshakable, even in times of trouble:

You will never become angry or impatient if you love them for the sake of God...There are imperfections in every human being, and you will always become unhappy if you look toward the people themselves. But if you look toward God you will love them and be kind to them, for the world of God is the world of perfection and complete mercy.[174]   'Abdu'l-Bahá

The attribute that links our soul with God—loyalty or faithfulness—must also link the lovers to each other in marriage. The most evident and essential sign of loyalty is chastity.[175]

The brightness of the light of chastity sheddeth its illumination upon the worlds of the spirit, and its fragrance is wafted even unto the Most Exalted Paradise...[176]   Bahá'u'lláh

Let your eye be chaste, your hand faithful, your tongue truthful and your heart enlightened.[177]

Bahá'u'lláh

Shoghi Effendi, the Guardian of the Bahá'í Faith, offers this clear guidance on the "proper use of the sex instinct:"

The proper use of the sex instinct is the natural right of every individual, and it is precisely for this very purpose that the institution of marriage has been established. The Bahá'ís do not believe in the suppression of the sex impulse but in its regulation and control.[178]

Bahá'u'lláh declares:

And if he [My true follower] met the fairest and most comely of women, he would not feel his heart seduced by the least shadow of desire for her beauty. Such a soul indeed is the creation of spotless chastity. Thus instructeth you the Pen of the Ancient of Days, as bidden by your Lord, the Almighty, the All-Bountiful.[179]

In the Bahá'í Faith, the education of children is given the highest priority:

The education and training of children is among the most meritorious acts of humankind and draweth down the grace and favor of the All-Merciful, for education is the indispensable foundation of all human excellence...[180] 'Abdu'l-Bahá

If, in this momentous task, a mighty effort be exerted, the world of humanity will...shed the fairest light. Then will this darksome place grow luminous, and this abode of earth turn into Heaven.[181] 'Abdu'l-Bahá

You must attach the greatest importance to the education of children, for this is the foundation of the Law of God, and the bedrock of the edifice of His Faith.[182] 'Abdu'l-Bahá

The instruction of these children is even as the work of a loving gardener who tendeth his young plants in the flowering fields of the All-Glorious. There is no doubt that it will yield the desired results...the little children must needs be made aware in their very heart and soul that "Bahá'í" is not just a name but a truth. Every child must be trained in the things of the spirit, so that he may embody all the virtues and become a source of glory to the Cause of God. Otherwise, the mere word "Bahá'í," if it yield no fruit, will come to nothing.

Strive then to the best of thine ability to let these children know that a Bahá'í is one who embodieth all the perfections...[183]   'Abdu'l-Bahá

How Do Bahá'ís Reconcile Religion and Science?

If religious beliefs and opinions are found contrary to the standards of science, they are mere superstitions...Unquestionably there must be agreement between true religion and science. If a question be found contrary to reason, faith and belief in it are impossible, and there is no outcome but wavering and vacillation.[184]   'Abdu'l-Bahá

Science reveals the truths and mysteries of the physical world; religion those of the spiritual. Each concerns itself with a separate but interdependent dimension of the universe. Seldom do the sacred Scriptures address scientific issues. Exceptions are few. For instance, a Qur'ánic verse declares that the sun is a flowing and stationary body (Qur'án 36:37-38; see also *Some Answered Questions*, Chapter 7).

This knowledge contradicted the prevailing view of the time. Scientists also, as a rule, avoid involvement in religious issues.

Why, then, does conflict occur? It occurs mostly from mistaking metaphoric messages for literal. Aside from their teachings, the sacred Scriptures are masterpieces of literature. They contain an abundance of "figures of speech." Understanding the symbolism behind literary figures requires imagination and openness. Dogmatic believers, who often present themselves as the only model of true faith and understanding, are quite literal-minded.

This *seemingly* harmless and trivial handicap leads to devastating consequences. First, it causes a rift between religion and science and thereby destroys religion's dignity in the eyes of enlightened believers and seekers of truth; and second, it prevents people from understanding the symbolic meaning of prophecies, which in turn leads to the denial of divine Messengers. Once again we see the role of dogmatic believers in creating misconceptions and stifling truth and understanding on a vast scale.

Religion is like a glass of pure water. Conflicting theological theories have filled it with so many pollutants that the water has become a source of disease. Bahá'u'lláh gives us a fresh glass of water.

Theology, as practiced, is the art of turning simple ideas into obscure theories. "And Jesus said, 'Who do you say I am?' And a theologian answered, 'You are the eschatological manifestation of the ground of our being, the kerygma in which we found the ultimate meaning of our life.' And Jesus said, 'What?'"

In His *Book of Certitude*, Bahá'u'lláh quotes this passage:

> Knowledge is one point, which the foolish have multiplied.[185]

Is Human Nature Good or Evil?

> We who lived in the concentration camps can remember the men who walked through the huts comforting others, giving away their last piece of bread. They may have been few in numbers, but they offer sufficient proof that everything can be taken from a man but one thing: The last of his freedoms—to choose one's attitude in any given set of circumstances, to choose one's own way.
>
> Viktor Frankl

The theological portrayal of human nature has been predominantly negative. Instead of reminding us of the supreme honor of being made in God's image, of being the essence of beauty and perfection, many theologians focus on our sinful nature and remind us of our rebellious past when Adam and Eve reached for the forbidden fruit. As Dr. David Elkind, a noted child psychologist observes, "The Puritans constructed an image of the child tainted with original sin. 'Your child,' wrote James Janeway, 'is never too young to go to hell.'"[186]

"A pastor was talking to an enthusiastic, but ignorant member of his flock. 'My friend, I assume you believe in total depravity?' the preacher asked. The man answered, 'Yes, sir, and what a worthy doctrine it would be, if only folks would live up to it.'"

The reason for ignoring the good and focusing on the bad is this: If people were good, it is assumed, then they would not need Christ's salvation. This thinking is totally unfounded. When we say that human beings are made perfect, we mean *potentially* perfect. Just like a photograph, God's image imprinted on their souls needs to be developed. Without His help, the splendid and exalted image breaks down and disappears. The perfect seed always needs a cultivator, otherwise it rots. Christ said that the kingdom of heaven is concealed within every human being. That perfect kingdom always needs a King. Without the King, only chaos can prevail.

Christ said that a good fruit can come only from a good tree and a bad fruit only from a bad tree. Since God is good, everything that comes from Him—the creation—also must be good.

Among all created beings we are the only ones made in God's image. We are the only ones with souls that reflect His Soul. Can a perfect Being have an evil image? Can any honor compare with being like the Essence of all Beauty and Perfection? Can we ever be grateful enough for receiving such an unspeakably magnificent gift? In spite of this, we find so many people completely unaware of the great honor and glory of being human. Many suffer from a low self-esteem. They have the power to connect their souls to the Source of all joys and pleasures, yet they remain deprived and depressed.

Theirs are the most sublime riches and gifts of God's kingdom, yet they live in poverty. Christ said that "the kingdom of heaven is within you." Can anything good and beautiful be lacking in "the kingdom of heaven"? The best of everything that the mind can conceive dwells within us. We are, indeed, made perfect.

When God created us, He was pleased with His work and He called it good (Genesis 1:10, 12, 18, 21, 25, 31). Then where does the bad come from? God fashioned us first as a blank film, and then exposed it to His image. But He left the task of developing the film to us. The bad always comes from a lack of development, and that is perhaps the main message in the story of Adam and Eve. That story does not point to an existing innate evil in human beings. Rather, it symbolizes a sublime gift given to human beings: freedom of choice. If that gift were removed, we would become mere animals.

Only when we expose ourselves to the light of the knowledge of God, as manifested in His great Messengers, can we reveal our souls' inner beauty and perfection. When we deny His Messengers and reject His knowledge, we remain in an unsightly and negative state.

Today we are constantly exposed to bad news—war, crime, child abuse, fraud, infidelity, and cruelty of all kinds. The negative is seldom neutralized by the positive. This abundance of bad news creates a bad image of humans. Since we live up to our self-image, when our attention is drawn to the negative, our image of being human declines. And as our image goes down, so do our values and our sense of honor and dignity. As humorist Will Rogers said, "God made man a little lower than the angels, and he has been getting a little lower ever since."

What we see is not what we are. Without cultivating our souls, we descend to a state lower than that of lizards and lions, and worse than wasps and wolves. If you owned a hotel, whom would you prefer as a guest, a dog or a dishonest drunkard? "A man wrote this letter to a small hotel he planned to visit on his vacation: 'I would very much like to bring my dog with me. He is well-groomed and very well-behaved. Would you be willing to let me keep him in my room with me at night?'

An immediate reply came from the hotel owner, who said, 'I've been operating this hotel for many years. In all that time, I've never had a dog steal towels, silverware, or pictures off the walls. I've never had to evict a dog in the middle of the night for being drunk and disorderly. And I've never had a dog run out on a hotel bill. Yes, indeed, your dog is welcome at my hotel. And, if your dog will vouch for you, you're welcome to stay here, too.'"

A mother went to the school open house to speak with her son's teacher. The teacher said, "I'm so very pleased to meet you. Your son Tim is a delight to have in my class! He's helpful, conscientious, courteous..."

Tim's mother wondered: "My kid? Is she talking about *my* kid?" Later she told Tim: "Your teacher says you are delightful! Why can't you be that good at home?" Tim replied, "Mom, I've only got so much goodness to go around!"

Tim had a lot of potential for both good and evil. He selected and gave to each person what he or she expected of him.

How do we treat gold and garbage? We keep one, and throw the other away. That principle applies to how we perceive ourselves. If we think we are made by God and for God, we glow and glitter like gold, and our self-appreciation ascends as high as the angels. If we think we were made by chance for the grave and grubs, our self-worth descends like an unopened parachute, crashing to the ground. As the Book of Proverbs declares, "As a man thinketh, so is he."

Once again, we need to restore to our souls the glory and honor of being human, of being made in the Creator's image. These quotations from 'Abdu'l-Bahá express our true station:

> Man is the sum of Creation, and the Perfect Man is the expression of the complete thought of the Creator—the Word of God.[187] Of all the created beings man is the nearest to the nature of God...[188] Man is the highest work of creation, the nearest to God of all creatures.[189]

Bahá'u'lláh showers upon us every honor imaginable. He elevates us to the rank of the angels. He declares that God has put within each of us the very essence of His light,[190] that we are the very purpose and fruit of all creation, the reason for which the universe came into being.

We need to be constantly reminded of our splendid destiny and the infinite riches the Creator has placed within each of us.

O SON OF BEING!
Thou art My lamp and My light is in thee. Get thou from it thy radiance and seek none other than Me. For I have created thee rich and have bountifully shed My favor upon thee.[191]

Bahá'u'lláh

O SON OF BEING!
With the hands of power I made thee and with the fingers of strength I created thee; and within thee have I placed the essence of My light. Be thou content with it and seek naught else, for My work is perfect and My command is binding. Question it not, nor have a doubt thereof.[192]

Bahá'u'lláh

O SON OF SPIRIT!
I created thee rich, why dost thou bring thyself down to poverty? Noble I made thee, wherewith dost thou abase thyself? Out of the essence of knowledge I gave thee being, why seekest thou enlightenment from anyone beside Me? Out of the clay of love I molded thee, how dost thou busy thyself with another? Turn thy sight unto thyself, that thou mayest find Me standing within thee, mighty, powerful and self-subsisting.[193]

Bahá'u'lláh

This statement from the Báb shows God's infinite love for human beings:

All things have been created for your sakes, and for the sake of naught else hath your creation been ordained.[194]

The Báb

Spiritually and emotionally we are living in a hostile age. The prevalence of mental disorder in our time is a symptom of deficiencies and pressures within us. We are like ships at the mercy of the winds and the waves. At this time in history, the best we can do is simply to stay afloat. To accomplish this, we must first make sure that the ship is strong and will not break down in the storms; second, we must have a goal, a sense of direction, so that we know we are not lost.

The strength of the ship is our sense of self-worth. It is having faith that, in spite of our weakness, *we are good*, we are God-made; it is believing that we are noble, worthy of preserving, not for the grave but for God, not for a few seasons but for all eternity. To have any value, this sense of self-worth must be crowned with a purpose. That purpose for every human being is to grow, to manifest one's inner perfections, to become worthy of God, and to attain His presence.

It is absolutely essential for every human being to meet both of these needs. For our spiritual survival, they are as essential as air is for our physical. Without them, we are no more than dead bodies floating on the sea.

If parents provide an example of self-worth and a sense of passionate purpose for life, it is hard to imagine that a child would consider suicide as an alternative. People kill themselves for many reasons. But at the root of every suicide lies the lack of a strong sense of self-worth and purpose, which should be instilled early in life. If religion fails to provide both these needs, it is pseudo-religion.

The Bahá'í view of human nature has a profound impact on the way children think about themselves and relate to others. It teaches them to respect every human being. Is it possible to view people as God's masterpieces, and yet fail to respect them? Our awareness of our divine essence affects every aspect of our lives, but is best demonstrated in the way we relate to others. In the light of that knowledge, people become precious to us. We consider it a supreme honor to be in the presence of beings whom God describes as "the essence of My light." Like a beam of light, our attitude toward others always reflects back to us and helps us appreciate God's immortal gifts and His presence in our own souls.

Are Bahá'ís Active in Improving the Socio-Economic State of the World?

The Bahá'í Faith combines the mystical and the practical. It teaches world-mindedness and concern for all members of the human race. Love is not just a feeling. True love, like electricity, generates powers called service and self-sacrifice:

> That one indeed is a man who, today, dedicateth himself to the service of the entire human race.[195]
>
> Bahá'u'lláh

A report by UNICEF indicates that one fifth of the world's population lives in abject poverty. The disparity between rich and poor nations offers abundant opportunities for socio-economic service. This prophecy is about our time:

> Open your eyes and look at the fields. They are ripe for harvest!
>
> Christ (John 4:35)

Bahá'ís currently manage over 1,300 development projects. The majority of them are the result of grassroots efforts operating with little or no outside support.

Activities in health, social services, communications, agriculture, forestry, and community development encourage work in the spirit of service to humankind. The emphasis in Bahá'í teachings on the necessity of universal education has inspired the establishment of more than 900 tutorial schools and training centers in Africa, Asia, and the Americas. Bahá'í communities operate 29 formal primary and secondary schools. The figures will continue to increase in the years to come.

Social and economic development projects worldwide also include medical centers, programs for women, cooperative savings programs, building renovation, arts and theater groups, communal farms, cooperative fishing projects, homes for refugees and for the aged, and computer education to assist low income families.

Seven educational radio stations currently operate in Liberia, Panama, Chile, Peru, Bolivia, Ecuador and the United States, to serve the local populations. Programs in native languages offer information on health care, crop management, animal husbandry, child development, the elimination of prejudice, and the equality of men and women.[196]

The spiritual teachings of Bahá'u'lláh emphasize self-reliance and self-sufficiency, and they promote a holistic and world-embracing approach in understanding social problems and their underlying causes...For example, efforts to alleviate poverty cannot be divorced from activities that promote full equality for women. The vast majority of the world's poor are women and children. In many developing countries, especially in Africa, women farmers grow much of the food. Bahá'ís believe that efforts to ensure food security in these regions depend largely on improvements to the status of women. Issues of development and environment are equally dependent on finding solutions to problems of racism, under-education and religious strife.[197]

The recent trend in the distribution of wealth in many industrial nations, if continued, will lead to grave consequences. It is contrary to one of the most fundamental teachings of Bahá'u'lláh: an equitable distribution of wealth. To get a clear picture of what is happening in our time, read *America: What Went Wrong?* by two Pulitzer Prize-winning authors. For their book they did two years of research and assembled over 100,000 pages of documents to create "a gripping portrayal of the painful dismantling of the American middle class." This brief excerpt from the book gives a glimpse of the economic trends:

Between 1980 and 1989, the combined salaries of people in the $20,000 to $50,000 income group increased 44 percent. During the same period, the combined salaries of people earning $1 million or more a year increased, 2,184 percent.

Viewed more broadly, the total wages of all people who earned less than $50,000 a year—85 percent of all Americans—increased an average of just 2 percent a year over those ten years. At the same time, the total wages of all millionaires shot up 243 percent a year. Those figures are not adjusted for inflation, which cuts across all income groups but hits the lower and middle classes hardest.

Between 1980 and 1989, the number of people reporting incomes of more than a half-million dollars rocketed from 16,881 to 183,240—an increase of 985 percent.[198]

According to *Nightline* (October 27, 1995), since 1973, the yearly income of the poorest people in America has dropped by $1,300, while the yearly income of the richest has climbed by $66,000. The shift in wealth, the report stated, began in 1973.

One way Bahá'ís try to improve the socio-economic state of the world is through the United Nations:

The Bahá'í International Community has consultative status with the United Nations Economic and Social Council and with the United Nations Children's Fund. It is also affiliated with the United Nations Environment Program and the UN Office of Public Information. It has representatives with the United Nations in New York, Geneva, and Nairobi. Local Bahá'í communities are encouraged to support the UN's various humanitarian projects. The Bahá'í International Community participates in meetings of UN agencies concerned with human rights, social development, the status of women, the environment, human settlement, food, science and technology, population, the law of the sea, crime prevention, substance abuse, youth, children, the family, disarmament, and the United Nations University.[199]

Sometimes, poverty persists because of a lack of motivation to work and earn a living. In God's sight, idleness diminishes our worth:

O MY SERVANT!
The basest of men are they that yield no fruit on earth. Such men are verily counted as among the dead, nay better are the dead in the sight of God than those idle and worthless souls.[200] Bahá'u'lláh

Bahá'í Writings elevate work done in a spirit of service to the rank of worship. The true purpose of working is not to make money but to serve others. "A wealthy man in Mexico was in the habit of buying two tangerines daily from a woman who operated a fruit stand near his house. One morning he told her he wanted to buy her entire stock of tangerines. Much to his surprise the lady refused to sell him more than a few. 'But why?' the buyer asked. 'If I sold you all of my tangerines,' she answered with dignity, 'what would I do the rest of the day?'"

Do Bahá'ís Pray?

Bahá'ís have a spiritual obligation to pray every day. Why should we pray? To express our love, gratitude, and devotion to our supreme and ever-lasting Lover, to seek spiritual guidance, to remind ourselves of our immortal essence and destiny, and to strengthen our souls against the pressures of daily living. If we truly love someone, would we not call on him or her every day? Then how can we love God without remembering Him and talking to Him? Calling our true Lover and Beloved is the only long-distance call that is free, never busy, jammed, out of order, or under the control of a soulless recorder. God asks us to keep in touch, He loves to hear our voices: "Call on Me and I will answer thee" (Jeremiah 33:3). God answers our sincere prayers every time, but not always the way we expect.

At the dawn of every day he [the true seeker] should commune with God, and, with all his soul, persevere in the quest of his Beloved. He should consume every wayward thought with the flame of His loving mention.[201]   Bahá'u'lláh

Yield ye praise then unto Him and glorify Him and bear ye witness to the sanctity and oneness of His Being and magnify His might and majesty with wondrous glorification. This will enable you to gain admittance into the all-highest Paradise. Would that ye had firm faith in the revelation of the signs of God.[202]   The Báb

We should speak in the language of heaven—in the language of the spirit—for there is a language of the spirit and heart. It is as different from our language as our own language is different from that of the animals, who express themselves only by cries and sounds.

It is the language of the spirit which speaks to God. When, in prayer, we are freed from all outward things and turn to God, then it is as if in our hearts we hear the Voice of God. Without words we speak, we communicate, we converse with God and hear the answer...All of us, when we attain to a truly spiritual condition, can hear the Voice of God.[203]

'Abdu'l-Bahá

We should pray not out of fear but out of love:

In the highest prayer, men pray only for the love of God, not because they fear Him or hell, or hope for bounty or heaven...When a man falls in love with a human being, it is impossible for him to keep from mentioning the name of his beloved. How much more difficult is it to keep from mentioning the Name of God when one has come to love Him...The spiritual man finds no delight in anything save in commemoration of God.[204]

'Abdu'l-Bahá

In the Bahá'í Scriptures, we find several volumes of prayers. This is an example of a daily prayer:

I bear witness, O my God, that Thou hast created me to know Thee and to worship Thee. I testify, at this moment, to my powerlessness and to Thy might, to my poverty and to Thy wealth. There is none other God but Thee, the Help in Peril, the Self-Subsisting.[205]

Bahá'u'lláh

A prayer for those in difficulties:

Is there any Remover of difficulties save God? Say: Praised be God! He is God! All are His servants, and all abide by His bidding![206]

The Báb

A morning prayer:

I have awakened in Thy shelter, O my God, and it becometh him that seeketh that shelter to abide within the Sanctuary of Thy Protection...Illumine my inner being, O my Lord, with the splendors of the Dayspring of Thy Revelation, even as Thou didst illumine my outer being with the morning light of Thy favor.[207]   *Bahá'u'lláh*

A prayer for tranquillity:

O God! Refresh and gladden my spirit. Purify my heart. Illumine my powers. I lay all my affairs in Thy hand. Thou art my Guide and my Refuge. I will no longer be sorrowful and grieved; I will be a happy and joyful being. O God! I will no longer be full of anxiety, nor will I let trouble harass me. I will not dwell on the unpleasant things of life.

O God! Thou art more friend to me than I am to myself. I dedicate myself to Thee, O Lord.[208]
'Abdu'l-Bahá

A prayer to express love for God:

O my God! O my God! This, Thy servant, hath advanced towards Thee, is passionately wandering in the desert of Thy love, walking in the path of Thy service, anticipating Thy favors, hoping for Thy bounty, relying upon Thy kingdom, and intoxicated by the wine of Thy gift. O my God! Increase the fervor of his affection for Thee, the constancy of his praise of Thee, and the ardor of his love for Thee.

Verily, Thou art the Most Generous, the Lord of grace abounding. There is no other God but Thee, the Forgiving, the Merciful.[209]   *'Abdu'l-Bahá*

A prayer seeking assistance:

O Thou Whose face is the object of my adoration, Whose beauty is my sanctuary, Whose habitation is my goal, Whose praise is my hope, Whose providence is my companion, Whose love is the cause of my being, Whose mention is my solace, Whose nearness is my desire, Whose presence is my dearest wish and highest aspiration, I entreat Thee not to withhold from me the things Thou didst ordain for the chosen ones among Thy servants. Supply me, then, with the good of this world and of the next.

Thou, truly, art the King of all men. There is no God but Thee, the Ever-Forgiving, the Most Generous.[210]   *Bahá'u'lláh*

A prayer for healing:

Thy name is my healing, O my God, and remembrance of Thee is my remedy. Nearness to Thee is my hope, and love for Thee is my companion. Thy mercy to me is my healing and my succor in both this world and the world to come. Thou, verily, art the All-Bountiful, the All-Knowing, the All-Wise.[211]   *Bahá'u'lláh*

A prayer praising God:

I beg Thee to forgive me, O my Lord, for every mention but the mention of Thee, and for every praise but the praise of Thee, and for every delight but delight in Thy nearness, and for every pleasure

*but the pleasure of communion with Thee, and
for every joy but the joy of Thy love and of Thy
good-pleasure, and for all things pertaining unto
me which bear no relationship unto Thee, O Thou
Who art the Lord of lords, He Who provideth the
means and unlocketh the doors.*[212]   *The Báb*

Praying and the reading of Scriptures should be
done with joy and in moderation:

Pride not yourselves on much reading of the
verses...Were a man to read a single verse with
joy and radiance it would be better for him than
to read with lassitude all the Holy Books of
God.[213]   Bahá'u'lláh

The most acceptable prayer is the one offered
with the utmost spirituality and radiance; its
prolongation hath not been and is not beloved by
God. The more detached and the purer the prayer,
the more acceptable is it in the presence of
God.[214]   The Báb

"A pastor asked a little girl what she thought of her
first experience in a meeting of 'holy rollers,'
where they praised the Lord for hours at a time.
'The music was nice,' she said, 'but the commercial
was too long.'"

If one friend feels love for another, he will wish
to say so. Though he knows that the friend is
aware that he loves him, he will still wish to say
so...God knows the wishes of all hearts, but the
impulse to pray is a natural one, springing from
man's love to God...

If this love and desire are lacking, it is useless to try and force them. Words without love mean nothing. If a person talks to you as an unpleasant duty, with no love or pleasure in his meeting with you, do you wish to converse with him?[215]

'Abdu'l-Bahá

What Are the Sacred Scriptures of the Bahá'í Faith?

The flowers fade, but the word of our God endures for evermore. Isaiah 40:8

Never before has such an abundance of Scriptures been entrusted to humankind. Because of the greatness of this day, the Word of God has poured forth like a torrent.

For the first time in religious history, we have reliable evidence of how the Word of God is revealed. Several independent observers have testified that sometimes the Báb and Bahá'u'lláh spoke the divine Words with such speed that no one could write them down. *The Book of Certitude* (257 pages), which resolves the mysteries of past Scriptures, was written by Bahá'u'lláh within the span of only two days.

Authors make corrections, change their minds, modify their styles, and mature with time. Like a candle's flame before the wind, their thoughts flicker and flutter, and die with little impact on their surroundings.

The Word of God radiates like the sun with unmatched splendor, beauty, and perfection to the farthest reaches of the earth. It is the source of the spiritual life of the world. The winds and whims of time can never touch it.

> Thy word is a lamp unto my feet, and a light unto my path.   Psalms 119:105

Kahlil Gibran, the famous author from Lebanon, whose book *The Prophet* has been hailed as a classic, made this statement about Bahá'u'lláh's Arabic works, a language Bahá'u'lláh did not study:

> He [Kahlil Gibran] said it was the most stupendous literature that ever was written, and that He even coined words. That there was no Arabic that even touched the Arabic of Bahá'u'lláh.[216]

In the Bahá'í archives are treasured more than 15,000 Tablets or Epistles written by Bahá'u'lláh to His disciples.[217] If we assume that each of those Epistles is an average of three pages long, we have a total of about 45,000 pages. If 450 pages are put in each volume, we end up with 100 volumes. Each of those 15,000 Epistles reveals a glimpse of God's glory, perfection, and power. Each of those Epistles expresses His unwavering and unfailing love for humanity. And each of them manifests unparalleled authority, beauty, and majesty. I have had the honor of reading about 2,000 of those Epistles in the original language of revelation. Each time I read a new Epistle, my astonishment grows. Reading them is like walking through a splendid mansion adorned with majestic and precious pearls and jewels.

Those who witnessed the revelation of these sacred writings have testified that they were spoken as fast as they could be recorded. Secretaries could hardly keep up with the speed with which the words were uttered. What is even more astonishing is that they required no correction, modification, or change of any kind.

All sacred Scriptures testify to the supreme station of the Word of God:

> The words which I have spoken to you are both spirit and life. Christ (John 6:63)

> And the words of the Lord are flawless, like silver refined in a furnace of clay, purified seven times. Psalms 18:30

Both the Báb and Bahá'u'lláh declare repeatedly that their Words are the surest evidence of their divine distinction:

> He, the divine King, hath proclaimed the un-disputed supremacy of the verses of His Book over all things that testify to His truth. For compared with all other proofs and tokens, the divinely-revealed verses shine as the sun, whilst all others are as stars. To the peoples of the world they are the abiding testimony, the incontro-vertible proof, the shining light of the ideal King. Their excellence is unrivaled, their virtue nothing can surpass. They are the treasury of the divine pearls and the depository of the divine mysteries.[218] Bahá'u'lláh

> Indeed these manifest verses are conclusive testimony for those who seek true guidance.[219]
> The Báb

Certainly God's way of thinking and speaking must be distinct from ours—as distinct and exalted as the heavens are from the earth:

> "For my thoughts are not your thoughts, neither are your ways my ways," declares the Lord. "As the heavens are higher than the earth, so are my ways higher than your ways and my thoughts than your thoughts."   Isaiah 55:8-9

Whenever you examine the Writings of the Báb and Bahá'u'lláh, remember that they were spoken as quickly as the secretaries could record. No human being, other than the One endowed and inspired by God, can claim such distinction. The most talented, seasoned, and skillful authors cannot produce, spontaneously and without pause, even as much as one page that would come close, in beauty and novelty, to the works of the Báb and Bahá'u'lláh—neither of whom had any education. When we add the dimension of meaning to the dimension of language, we get peerless pearls of celestial perfection.

The Word of God, spoken through His great Messengers, is the mightiest miracle. It is not like a meteor that flashes forth and dies in the moments of history. It is a celestial magic that endures for all generations. It is as bright and enduring as the sun, as ever-present as the universe itself. No evidence, no proof can ever compare with it.

It seems God puts most or all of His miracles in His Word. Consider the Báb. He began His ministry at the age of 25. He had hardly any education. As far as we know, He did not even finish elementary school. His teacher sent Him home, saying that the child knew much more than he did. Imagine a young man, raised in an extremely regressive and repressive culture, who arises with the most incredible news and reveals Scriptures as fast as anyone can write, in the most magnificent and exquisite style, in a language other than His mother tongue—one that He has never studied! What greater miracle does anyone need? This is an ever-present wonder that we can witness any time we wish. This is the evidence God wants us to depend on.

How could the Israelites endure so much pain in the desert? What gave them the strength and courage was the "manna," the food from heaven. That food symbolized the Word of God. (See John 6:30-58.)

To observe brevity, only a few brief selections from the vast vineyard of Bahá'í sacred works are offered here. It is essential for every seeker of truth to devote much time to the study of those sources.

The Báb and 'Abdu'l-Bahá also wrote extensively. Their works also constitute part of Bahá'í sacred Scriptures. Here are a few references in English:

By Bahá'u'lláh

Gleanings from the Writings of Bahá'u'lláh
The Hidden Words of Bahá'u'lláh
The Seven Valleys and the Four Valleys
The Book of Certitude
Prayers and Meditations by Bahá'u'lláh
The Proclamation of Bahá'u'lláh
Tablets of Bahá'u'lláh

By the Báb

Selections from the Writings of the Báb

By 'Abdu'l-Bahá

Some Answered Questions
Selections from the Writings of 'Abdu'l-Bahá
The Secret of Divine Civilization
The Promulgation of Universal Peace
Paris Talks

The following quotations, selected by Shoghi Effendi, the Guardian of the Bahá'í Faith, from Bahá'í Scriptures, are inscribed over the alcoves and entrances to the Bahá'í House of Worship in Wilmette, Illinois. Each of them is like a facet of diamond harvested from the vast mountains of celestial jewels. As you read, ponder in your heart the meaning of each jewel:

All the prophets of God proclaim the same faith.

Religion is a radiant light and an impregnable stronghold.

Ye are the fruits of one tree, and the leaves of one branch.

So powerful is unity's light that it can illumine the whole earth.

Consort with the followers of all religions with friendliness.

O Son of Being! Thou art My lamp and My light is in thee.

O Son of Being! Walk in My statutes for love of Me.

Thy Paradise is My love; thy heavenly home reunion with Me.

The light of a good character surpasseth the light of the sun.

The earth is but one country, and mankind its citizens.

The best beloved of all things in My sight is Justice; turn not away therefrom if thou desirest Me.

My love is My stronghold; he that entereth therein is safe and secure.

Breathe not the sins of others so long as thou art thyself a sinner.

Thy heart is My home; sanctify it for My descent.

I have made death a messenger of joy to thee. Wherefore dost thou grieve?

Make mention of Me on My earth, that in My heaven I may remember thee.

O rich ones on earth! The poor in your midst are My trust; guard ye My trust.

The source of all learning is the knowledge of God, exalted be His Glory.[220]

The Scriptures of a religion are its very heart and soul. They come not from human beings, but from the heart of heaven. They are the hallmark of God's Messengers, the most evident sign of their greatness. Anyone interested in knowing Bahá'u'lláh should study His writings diligently. He invites the seekers of truth again and again to test Him by His works—by the heavenly fruits He bears. As Christ declared, a tree must be judged by its fruits. If the fruits are good, the tree must be good.

Love is the greatest law in the universe. It is the light of the world. Here are a few fruits from the vineyard of Bahá'u'lláh's and 'Abdu'l-Bahá's works on love:

Love is the source of all the bestowals of God. Until love takes possession of the heart, no other divine bounty can be revealed in it.[221]   'Abdu'l-Bahá

Order your lives in accordance with the first principle of divine teaching, which is love.[222]

'Abdu'l-Bahá

In the garden of thy heart plant naught but the rose of love.[223]   *Bahá'u'lláh*

To every human being must ye be infinitely kind.[224]

'Abdu'l-Bahá

Look not upon the creatures of God except with the eye of kindliness and mercy, for Our loving providence hath pervaded all created things, and Our grace encompasseth the earth and the heavens.[225]

Bahá'u'lláh

You must have infinite love for each other, each preferring the other before himself.[226]   'Abdu'l-Bahá

You must love your friend better than yourself; yes, be willing to sacrifice yourself...I desire that you be ready to sacrifice everything for each other, even life itself.[227]   'Abdu'l-Bahá

Blessed is he who prefers his brother before himself.[228]   *Bahá'u'lláh*

A thought of hatred must be destroyed by a more powerful thought of love.[229]   'Abdu'l-Bahá

Think ye of love and good fellowship as the delights of heaven, think ye of hostility and hatred as the torments of hell.[230]   'Abdu'l-Bahá

Love the creatures for the sake of God and not for themselves. You will never become angry or impatient if you love them for the sake of God.[231]
'Abdu'l-Bahá

When a man turns his face to God he finds sun-shine everywhere...Do not be content with showing friendship in words alone, let your heart burn with loving-kindness for all who may cross your path.[232]
'Abdu'l-Bahá

Let them at all times concern themselves with doing a kindly thing for one of their fellows, offering to someone love, consideration, thoughtful help. Let them see no one as their enemy, or as wishing them ill, but think of all humankind as their friends; regarding the alien as an intimate, the stranger as a companion, staying free of prejudice, drawing no lines.[233]
'Abdu'l-Bahá

Ye were created to show love one to another and not perversity and rancor. Take pride not in love for yourselves but in love for your fellow-creatures. Glory not in love for your country, but in love for all mankind.[234]
Bahá'u'lláh

Love, in its fullness and purity, is the mother of all virtues. It is the power that gives birth to everything good and noble. It is the very purpose of human life.

Love, in its fullness, means seeking and embracing truth and goodness. Everything true is good, and everything good is true. God is truth and goodness. Love is truth and goodness. A person who loves truth and goodness understands that:

- There exists a just and caring God who must be known, loved, and glorified for His greatness

- Justice is better than cruelty

- Honesty excels dishonesty

- Knowledge is superior to ignorance

- Wisdom transcends folly

- Doing is nobler than simply sitting and dreaming.

Therefore "love is the great secret." When we have true love, we discover and live by truth and goodness; we have attained the purpose for which the universe came into being.

> *We love to see you at all times consorting in amity and concord...We shall always be with you; if We inhale the perfume of your fellowship, Our heart will assuredly rejoice, for naught else can satisfy Us.*[235]   *Bahá'u'lláh*

Let us conclude this section with two quotations on virtues, one by Christ, the other by Bahá'u'lláh:

> *Blessed are the poor in spirit, for theirs is the kingdom of heaven.*

> *Blessed are those who mourn, for they will be comforted.*

> *Blessed are the meek, for they will inherit the earth.*

> *Blessed are those who hunger and thirst for righteousness, for they will be filled.*

> *Blessed are the merciful, for they will be shown mercy.*

> *Blessed are the pure in heart, for they will see God.*

Blessed are the peacemakers, for they will be called sons of God.

Blessed are those who are persecuted because of righteousness, for theirs is the kingdom of heaven.

Christ (Matt. 5:3-10)

Be generous in prosperity, and thankful in adversity.

Be worthy of the trust of thy neighbor, and look upon him with a bright and friendly face.

Be a treasure to the poor, an admonisher to the rich, an answerer of the cry of the needy, a preserver of the sanctity of thy pledge.

Be fair in thy judgment, and guarded in thy speech.

Be unjust to no man, and show all meekness to all men.

Be as a lamp unto them that walk in darkness, a joy to the sorrowful, a sea for the thirsty, a haven for the distressed, an upholder and defender of the victim of oppression. Let integrity and uprightness distinguish all thine acts.

Be a home for the stranger, a balm to the suffering, a tower of strength for the fugitive.

Be eyes to the blind, and a guiding light unto the feet of the erring.

Be an ornament to the countenance of truth, a crown to the brow of fidelity, a pillar of the temple of righteousness, a breath of life to the body of mankind, an ensign of the hosts of justice, a luminary above the horizon of virtue, a dew to the soil of the human heart, an ark on the ocean of knowledge, a sun in the heaven of bounty, a gem on the diadem of wisdom, a shining light in the firmament of thy generation, a fruit upon the tree of humility.[236]   *Bahá'u'lláh*

Do Bahá'ís Believe in the Afterlife?

Without remembering, we have all made a journey from heaven to the earth, and now we are on the way back home.

All men have proceeded from God and unto Him shall all return. All shall appear before Him for judgment.[237]   The Báb

The dust returns to the ground it came from, and the spirit returns to God who gave it.

Ecclesiastes 12:7

O Lord, my soul shall live with thee; do thou give my spirit rest.   Isaiah 38:16

It is so easy to forget that we are travelers on a long journey, paying only a brief visit to the earth. It is so easy to forget that we are passengers on a spacecraft, that we have a chance to revolve around the sun a few times and then we must leave. We often get so attached to the spacecraft we don't want to go home. We should leave this world in the same spirit in which we arrived. When we came, we did not say "why or nay." Why should we complain when we are leaving for a better world?

Therefore it behooveth you to return unto God even as ye were brought forth into existence, and to utter not such words as why or nay, if ye wish your creation to yield fruit at the time of your return.[238]   The Báb

Our Creator, in expectation of our return to heaven, has prepared magnificent mansions with grand banquet halls. He wants us to get ready, to become pure, radiant, and fragrant. No one with a bad odor or sweaty clothes can enter the banquet. Its gates are quite sensitive to pollution; they simply do not open. Imagine if people with all kinds of odors and baggage entered the banquet! Then heaven would become as chaotic and polluted as the earth.

What happens to those who fail to prepare themselves for the banquet?

> Those who were ready went in with him to the wedding hall, and the door was closed. The other bridesmaids arrived later. "Lord, Lord," they said, "open the door for us," But he replied, "I tell you solemnly, I do not know you."
>
> Christ (Matt. 25:10-12)

Many of us lose hope and faith and can't see a reason for going through this life. Others can't wait; they want their rewards instantly. But our Creator asks us to be patient and faithful, and to keep reminding ourselves that the best is yet to come. "Art Linkletter told the children that 'life begins at forty' and asked the children if that were true. One little lad said: 'Life begins at three for me.' 'How's that?' Linkletter asked. 'Well, three is when school lets me out.'"

Those who have had near-death visions often report traveling through a dark tunnel, and then reaching the light. The tunnel symbolizes this life, the light the next life. To reach our destination, we must go through the tunnel, we must complete the journey—

experience sickness, pain, and death. "A little girl went to a doctor for a checkup and noticed the picture of an angel on the wall. 'What's that for?' the girl asked. 'That reminds me that someday I will go to heaven,' the doctor replied. 'Wouldn't you like to go to heaven?' 'Sure,' the girl answered. 'Well, what do you think we must do to get there?' the doctor asked. 'We must die first.' 'That's right,' the doctor smiled, 'but what must we do before that?' The girl pondered and then said, 'We must get sick and send for you!'"

> Heaven is blessed with perfect rest, but the blessing of the earth is toil.

While in this world, we have a choice to focus either on the light or on the tunnel. Only by looking up to the light does living and traveling in the tunnel make any sense. Only little children who die enjoy the privilege of getting to the light without going through the tunnel. And only our lack of faith and attachment to the world prevents us from recognizing this.

The awareness of our immortality keeps us from apathy, pessimism, and despair; or apathy, pessimism, and despair keep us from the awareness of our immortality.

Bahá'u'lláh teaches that the worlds of God are infinite, and that this life is the first stage among the infinite stages of our spiritual development. The transition from this life to the next does not result in the loss of any of our spiritual powers: our intelligence, our individuality, and the memory of our lives here. In fact, it results in the gaining of new and greater powers.

Now we see a poor reflection; then we shall see
face to face. Now I know in part; then I shall
know fully.   I Corinthians 13:12

The next world is far superior to this one, especially
for those who have lived a noble life on this plane
and have pleased the Lord. For them it is so
splendid, so grand and enchanting that, if they could
experience it, they would no longer wish to continue to live. They would deem this world a dark
and gloomy prison.

> Such is the station ordained for the true believer
> that if to an extent smaller than a needle's eye
> the glory of that station were to be unveiled to
> mankind, every beholder would be consumed
> away in his longing to attain it. For this reason
> it hath been decreed that in this earthly life the
> full measure of the glory of his own station
> should remain concealed from the eye of such a
> believer.[239]   Bahá'u'lláh

> Didst thou behold immortal sovereignty, thou
> wouldst strive to pass from this fleeting world.
> But to conceal the one from thee and to reveal
> the other is a mystery which none but the pure
> in heart can comprehend.[240]   Bahá'u'lláh

A friend asked: "How should one look forward to
death?" 'Abdu'l-Bahá answered:

> How does one look forward to the end of any
> journey? With hope and with expectation. It is
> even so with the end of this earthly journey.[241]

Bahá'u'lláh teaches that this realm is a place of
planting, not of harvesting; hence, we should not

always expect to receive the rewards of our good deeds here. He who plants a seed does not receive an instant harvest. God wishes us to show our trust in Him by being patient.

> Because you have seen me, you have believed; blessed are those who have not seen and yet have believed.   Christ (John 20:29)

"A wealthy man died and went to heaven. An angel took him on a guided tour of the celestial city. He came to a beautiful mansion. 'Who lives there?' asked the wealthy man. 'Oh,' the angel answered, 'on earth he was your servant.' The rich man got excited. If his servants lived this way, think of the kind of mansion he would have. Then they came to an even more magnificent mansion. 'Who's is this?' asked the rich man, almost overwhelmed. The angel answered, 'She spent her life teaching little children.' The rich man was really getting excited now. Finally they came to a tiny shack. It was the most modest home the rich man had ever seen. 'This is your home,' said the angel. The wealthy man began to cry. 'I'm sorry,' said the angel. 'We did all we could with what you sent us.'"

This world is a school and this life a test. If it weren't a test, we would have been subjected to binding controls and commands as are given to cats and crocodiles. Our prime purpose in the school of life is to get "a good report card."

> Teacher: "Johnny, give me a sentence with a direct object."
>
> Johnny: "Teacher, everybody thinks you're beautiful."

Teacher: "Thank you, Johnny, but what is the object?"

Johnny: "A good report card!"

In this school, we have the choice of being an honor student, a mediocre one, or a dropout. Whatever grade we receive here will be ours forever. In fact, our grade is the only thing we can carry beyond the grave. Have you ever seen anyone take gold to the grave? A man thought he could. Before his death, he told his friend, "People say you can't take anything with you, I am going to prove them wrong." Shortly before his death, he turned his wealth into cash, put the cash in three envelopes, gave one envelope to his friend, one to his lawyer, and one to his minister. In his will he specified that when his body was lowered to the grave, the three envelopes were to be dropped on to his coffin. His will was followed...but not quite. After the man was buried, the lawyer asked the other two if they had faithfully followed the will. The dead man's friend said, "Thoughts and thanks are more precious than money. Instead of cash, I put a thank-you note in his envelope." The lawyer said that he was not so wordy. He summarized his message in only three words. He wrote, "Are you kidding?" The minister said, "You both are so untrustworthy. I wrote him a personal check for the total amount!"

Some people are quite good at gambling with the gifts of life. They act like a man who went to a casino in a $50,000 Cadillac and returned on a $350,000 bus!

We are worth not as much as we have but as much as we are.

Most people spend their lives in pursuit of pleasures and possessions. The promise of paradise does not move them. They work hard for ephemeral palaces on earth, but not for eternal mansions in paradise. They devote their energies to be at the top of their graduating class in this world—a glamorous illusion that endures for but a little while and then vanishes. But when it comes to graduating from this world, their standards go down. "A student rushed into the office of his faculty advisor just after mid-terms, 'I need help!' The professor asked, 'What's your trouble?' The student replied, 'I got an F in science, an F in math, and a D in geography.' 'Well, what's your explanation for that?' asked the professor. The student replied, 'I think I spent too much time on geography!'"

Sacred Scriptures assure us that no learning however small, no act however insignificant, will be lost, that the One who has made the universe can certainly preserve our deeds and reward us accordingly.

> And if anyone gives a cup of cold water to one of these little ones...I tell you the truth, he will certainly not lose his reward.   Christ (Matt. 10:42)

Again, those who have had near-death visions indicate that:

- Death does not destroy the self, its sense of individuality, identity, or consciousness.

- The soul enters a new spiritual dimension, indescribable in its beauty and perfection.

- Physical pain and infirmity (blindness, deafness, etc.) disappear.

- The soul gains new gifts and powers, like the freedom to travel throughout the universe without any instrument, and to pass through physical barriers.

- The soul remembers and reviews all the events of its life, including caring or uncaring acts.

- There is some kind of evaluation of one's life.

- The soul has a chance to meet loved ones who have died.

- The individual returns with a sense of purpose and meaning for this life. He or she learns that the most critical goal in life is to love and to learn—to love all humanity (not just one's family members) and to seek knowledge.[242]

The following are a few brief quotes from people who have had near-death visions:

> "All pain vanished." "There was a feeling of utter peace and quiet, no fear at all." "After I came back, I cried off and on for about a week because I had to live in this world after seeing that one." "It opened up a whole new world for me...I kept thinking, 'There's so much that I've got to find out.'" "I heard a voice telling me what I had to do—go back—and I felt no fear."[243]

Bahá'í sacred writings on the afterlife are abundant. Here is an excerpt from Bahá'u'lláh's works:

> Thou hast asked Me concerning the nature of the soul. Know, verily, that the soul is a sign of God, a heavenly gem whose reality the most learned of men hath failed to grasp, and whose

mystery no mind, however acute, can ever hope to unravel. It is the first among all created things to declare the excellence of its Creator, the first to recognize His glory, to cleave to His truth, and to bow down in adoration before Him. If it be faithful to God, it will reflect His light, and will, eventually, return unto Him. If it fail, however, in its allegiance to its Creator, it will become a victim to self and passion, and will, in the end, sink in their depths.

Whoso hath, in this Day, refused to allow the doubts and fancies of men to turn him away from Him Who is the Eternal Truth, and hath not suffered the tumult provoked by the ecclesiastical and secular authorities to deter him from recognizing His Message, such a man will be regarded by God, the Lord of all men, as one of His mighty signs, and will be numbered among them whose names have been inscribed by the Pen of the Most High in His Book. Blessed is he that hath recognized the true stature of such a soul, that hath acknowledged its station, and discovered its virtues.[244]

In this world we see only the visible. Sometimes we doubt that we will ever enjoy the fruits of our labor. "One cold February day a snail started climbing an apple tree. As he inched slowly upward, a worm stuck its head from a crevice in the tree to offer some advice: 'You're wasting your energy. There isn't a single apple up there.' The snail kept up his slow climb. 'There will be when I get there,' he said."

Among the most beloved and blessed attributes in the sight of God is patience. Those who endure the unpleasant with resignation will receive "the choicest gifts:"

> Say, this earthly life shall come to an end, and everyone shall expire and return unto my Lord God Who will reward with the choicest gifts the deeds of those who endure with patience. Verily thy God assigneth the measure of all created things as He willeth, by virtue of His behest; and those who conform to the good-pleasure of your Lord, they are indeed among the blissful.[245]
>
> The Báb

We all know we can never get out of this world "alive." And yet we live as if we will. Life is a journey; we must consistently set goals and move on. What matters is not where we started but how far we have traveled. Our life is like a taxi ride. Whether we go anywhere or not, the meter keeps ticking. Sooner or later our earthly ride hits a dead end. And the ticking taxi has no reverse gears.

O CHILDREN OF NEGLIGENCE!
Set not your affections on mortal sovereignty and rejoice not therein. Ye are even as the unwary bird that with full confidence warbleth upon the bough; till of a sudden the fowler Death throws it upon the dust, and the melody, the form and the color are gone, leaving not a trace. Wherefore take heed, O bondslaves of desire![246] Bahá'u'lláh

All sacred Scriptures encourage us to take advantage of the opportunities we have in this life to advance spiritually. While here, on our journey towards God, we can advance in one instant as much as a thousand years. This will never again be possible. The most critical feature of this world among all the worlds of God is this: It sets the pace for everything that follows throughout all eternity. We are asked a thousand times and more to seize the moment before it is gone forever:

> Seize your chance...inasmuch as a fleeting moment in this Day excelleth centuries of a bygone age... Neither sun nor moon hath witnessed a day such as this.[247]   Bahá'u'lláh

> Hear and pay attention, do not be arrogant, for the Lord has spoken. Give glory to the Lord your God before he brings the darkness, before your feet stumble on the darkening hills. You hope for light but he will turn it to thick darkness and change it to deep gloom.   Jeremiah 13:15-16

> This is My counsel unto thee and unto the beloved of God. Whosoever wisheth, let him turn thereunto; whosoever wisheth, let him turn away. God, verily, is independent of him and of that which he may see and witness.[248]   Bahá'u'lláh

> This is what the Sovereign Lord says. Whoever will listen let him listen, and whoever will refuse let him refuse.   Ezekiel 3:27

O MOVING FORM OF DUST!

I desire communion with thee, but thou wouldst put no trust in Me...At all times I am near unto thee, but thou art ever far from Me. Imperishable glory I have chosen for thee, yet boundless

shame thou hast chosen for thyself. While there
is yet time, return, and lose not thy chance.[249]

Bahá'u'lláh

This day I call heaven and earth as witness...that
I have set before you life and death...Now choose
life...the Lord is your life...   Deuteronomy 3:19-20

And the Spirit and the bride say, Come. And let
him that heareth say, Come. And let him that is
athirst come. And whosoever will, let him take
the water of life freely.   Revelation 22:17

This world is a theater, where each of us presents
a concert. All the days of our lives should be
devoted to tuning our instruments and practicing so
that we can offer our heavenly Beloved the sweetest
melody. The state of the soul upon its departure is
our final melody. Once that moment has passed, we
will not have any chance of returning for a second
concert.

As long as it is day, we must do the work of him
who sent me. Night is coming, when no one can
work.   Christ (John 9:4)

The earth is not our permanent home. We must enjoy
this life and live it to its fullest but remain detached.
Nothing is ours. We don't even own ourselves:

Every living soul belongs to Me.   Ezekiel 18:4

As the Bahá'í burial ring reads:

We are God's and to Him shall we return.[250]

This world is a ladder, not a lazy chair. It was not
made for resting, but for reaching spiritual perfection. This planet is a place of learning and growing,
not of lying idle. Even if we own the whole world,

we must let go in the end. An old woman was hospitalized for a long time. She longed to be released from the hospital and to return home. Her wish was finally fulfilled, but not the way she expected. One day both her doctor and priest came to see her at the same time. She thought that this was the day of her release. The priest told her, "I have good news for you. You are such a wonderful person that your home is heaven." Her doctor said, "I have a bit of bad news, you will make the trip this Friday!"

Here is a piece of poetry from a small book titled *A Messenger of Joy*, about the afterlife:

> O my beloved friends! Gather blossoms of joy while you may. Hang your troubles upon the trees, and cast your cares to the wind.
>
> Banish the night with your love, wake the dawn with your praise.
>
> Sing and dance and be merry, but know there are other songs to sing.
>
> Live, but do not cling to your lives. Own, but do not be attached to your possessions.
>
> Cherish your pearls and rubies, let them dazzle your eyes, but know they are not yours. They belong to earth.
>
> Celebrate life, but be ready to depart the moment the banquet ends.
>
> When life bids you farewell, and death greets you, embrace her with open arms.[251]

Heaven is our great hope and our everlasting home. Some years ago a beautiful young actress was killed by a stalker in California. I saw the mother of the actress testify in the court. I heard her make this statement, "I wish I'd believed in heaven. Then I would know that I have a beautiful daughter in heaven. But I don't believe. And this creates this absence." There is a vacuum for heaven in every heart. Unless that vacuum is filled, life remains empty.

Although we know our Creator will reward us for good deeds, that should not be the reason for doing good. Dependency on rewards is a sign of immaturity. Children sometimes eat their dinner in the hope of getting a dessert. A mature person eats dinner for sheer enjoyment and health. To a spiritually advanced person, a good deed is its own reward. Anyone who is in harmony with God lives in heaven on earth.

> Those souls that, in this day, enter the divine kingdom and attain everlasting life, although materially dwelling on earth, yet in reality soar in the realm of heaven. Their bodies may linger on earth but their spirits travel in the immensity of space.[252]   'Abdu'l-Bahá

One way we can predict our spiritual position hereafter, as permanent residents in heaven, is to see how we have related to God and His creatures here as passing residents of the earth. Our Creator observes a simple rule of justice: He will treat us the way we treat Him and His creation. For instance, if we forgive others, He will forgive us; if we love Him, He will love us; if we are for Him, He will be for us; if we ignore His presence in His latest Manifestation or Messenger, He will ignore us; if we feel ashamed of the One He sends to save us, He will be ashamed of us:

> Whoever is ashamed of Me and My words...of him the Son of Man also will be ashamed when He comes in the glory of His Father [Glory of God].   Christ (Mark 8:38)

> God will verily do unto them that which they themselves are doing, and will forget them even as they have ignored His Presence in His day. Such is His decree unto those that have denied Him, and such will it be unto them that have rejected His signs.[253]   Bahá'u'lláh

By using this simple standard of "mutual treatment" here as citizens of the earthly kingdom, we can almost predict the state of our souls hereafter as citizens of the heavenly Kingdom.

Our Creator teaches us that this world is only a theater in which we choose the roles we prefer to play. To live in a physical world, we need and are given a physical form to carry us around. But the things that really matter are all invisible, spiritual. For the sake of observing the principle of diversity, the physical gifts are not equally distributed. But the spiritual gifts are put within the reach of every human being. No one is spiritually handicapped. No one can excuse himself by saying, "My father hated me, so I hated everybody else!" We are creatures of our cultures, but the masters of our souls. In God's sight, what matters is what is possible. *When we sincerely make an effort, when we listen and act without resorting to self-deception and excuses, His love enfolds us like a rainbow, His grace lifts us to the heavens on high.*

Belief in the afterlife and a constant awareness of our mortality elevates our perspective more than anything else. This is how one professor transforms his students' perspective:

> The death of a loved one, a severe illness, a financial setback, or extreme adversity can cause us to stand back, look at our lives, and ask ourselves some hard questions: "What's really important? Why am I doing what I'm doing?"... "Assume you only have this one semester to live," I tell my students, "and that during this semester you are to stay in school as a good student. Visualize how you would spend your semester."

> Things are suddenly placed in a different perspective. Values quickly surface that before weren't even recognized.

> I have also asked students to live with that expanded perspective for a week and keep a diary of their experiences.

> The results are very revealing. They start writing to parents to tell them how much they love and appreciate them. They reconcile with a brother, a sister, or a friend where the relationship has deteriorated.

> The dominant, central theme of their activities, the underlying principle, is love. The futility of badmouthing, bad thinking, put-downs, and accusation becomes very evident when they think in terms of having only a short time to live. Principles and values become more evident to everybody...

> When people seriously undertake to identify what really matters most to them in their lives, what they really want to be and to do, they become

very reverent. They start to think in larger terms than today and tomorrow.[254]

Here is a prayer from the Bahá'í sacred Writings for the departed:

He is God, exalted is He, the Lord of loving-kindness and bounty!...

O my God! Thou seest me detached from all save Thee, holding fast unto Thee and turning unto the ocean of Thy bounty, to the heaven of Thy favor, to the Daystar of Thy grace...

O my Lord! I myself and all created things bear witness unto Thy might, and I pray Thee not to turn away from Thyself this spirit that hath ascended unto Thee, unto Thy heavenly place, Thine exalted Paradise and Thy retreats of nearness, O Thou who art the Lord of all men!

Grant, then, O my God, that Thy servant may consort with Thy chosen ones, Thy saints and Thy Messengers in heavenly places that the pen cannot tell nor the tongue recount.

O My Lord, the poor one hath verily hastened unto the Kingdom of Thy wealth, the stranger unto his home within Thy precincts, he that is sore athirst to the heavenly river of Thy bounty. Deprive him not, O Lord, from his share of the banquet of Thy grace and from the favor of Thy bounty. Thou art in truth the Almighty, the Gracious, the All-Bountiful.

O my God, Thy Trust hath been returned unto Thee. It behooveth Thy grace and Thy bounty that have compassed Thy dominions on earth and in heaven, to vouchsafe unto Thy newly welcomed one Thy gifts and Thy bestowals, and the fruits of the tree of Thy grace! Powerful art Thou to do as Thou willest, there is none other God but Thee, the Gracious, the Most Bountiful, the Compassionate, the Bestower, the Pardoner, the Precious, the All-Knowing.

I testify, O my Lord, that Thou hast enjoined upon men to honor their guest, and he that hath ascended unto Thee hath verily reached Thee and attained Thy Presence. Deal with him then according to Thy grace and bounty! By Thy glory, I know of a certainty that Thou wilt not withhold Thyself from that which Thou hast commanded Thy servants, nor wilt Thou deprive him that hath clung to the cord of Thy bounty and hath ascended to the Dayspring of Thy wealth.

There is none other God but Thee, the One, the Single, the Powerful, the Omniscient, the Bountiful.[255]

Bahá'u'lláh

A Mission Statement

Many authors encourage their readers to write "a mission statement." The purpose of this project is to keep us focused and on track. The statement should be typed or printed attractively and be read every day. The reason for going through all this trouble is this: The world carries us forward like a mighty river with full force. It is so demanding, it takes every bit of energy we can muster just to stay afloat, just to cope with daily demands. The mission statement is like a tiny island in the midst of this fast-flowing river on which we can land for just a few moments every day to remind ourselves of the vast ocean at the end of the river.

"Justice Oliver Wendell Holmes once boarded a train in Washington, then promptly lost his ticket. The conductor recognized him and said, 'Never mind, Mr. Justice. When you find your ticket, I am certain you will mail it in.' 'Mr. Conductor,' replied Holmes, 'the question is not where is my ticket, but where am I supposed to be going?'"

According to author Stephen Covey, a mission statement accomplishes these purposes:

- It presents you with a circle of significance, a clear lens through which you can see the world.

- It serves as a personal constitution, as a standard by which you measure everything else in your life, as an expression of your vision and values.

- It gives you a sense of clarity, commitment, and freedom.

- It "forces you to think through your priorities deeply, carefully, and to align your behavior with your beliefs. Other people begin to sense that you're not being driven by everything that happens to you. You have a sense of mission about what you're trying to do and you are excited about it."[256]

It is never too late to learn and to start a new life.

Student: "I want to become a doctor."
Counselor: "Why don't you?"
Student: "It takes seven years. I will be an old man."
Counselor: "How old will you be in seven years if you ***don't*** go to school?"

It is possible to learn as late as the hour of death:

> How often hath a sinner attained, at the hour of death, to the essence of faith, and, quaffing the immortal draught, hath taken his flight unto the Concourse on high![257]   Bahá'u'lláh

It is also possible to unlearn at the hour of death:

> And how often hath a devout believer, at the hour of his soul's ascension, been so changed as to fall into the nethermost fire![258]   Bahá'u'lláh

Please take a few minutes to write a few lines or paragraphs below about what you want to accomplish most in the years and decades that are still yours. What is your most urgent purpose? What plans do you have to prepare yourself for your heavenly home? What specific steps will you take before your earthly journey is over?

My Mission Statement:

If you have difficulty composing a message, here is some help. Take any sentences you like from the following example:

My Mission in This Life, and My Eternal Destiny in the Life to Come

> There is a time when I must firmly choose the course I will follow, or the relentless drift of events will make all the decisions for me.

I am here as a guest; my true home is heaven. To enter, I must be clean and clothed, radiant and fragrant; otherwise I will be as bewildered and anxious as a first-grader who hesitated to go home. When the principal asked her why, she said, "Yesterday I left my expensive sweater at school. My Mommy told me not to come home without it. I don't know where she wants me to go!"

I am a spiritual being with an everlasting destiny. I am a soul with a body, not a body with a soul. I will be on earth for only a little while, but my brief stay here is more critical in determining my future destiny than the eternity that follows it. I recognize that all the roses of heaven lie in the seeds of this life.

My eternal home is heaven. My main mission in this life is to prepare my soul for that home. A consequence of that preparation is the profoundest and most enduring sense of fulfillment and happiness in this life.

What will it profit a man if he gains the whole world, and loses his own soul?   Christ (Mark 8:36)

What would it profit man, if he were to fail to recognize the Revelation of God? Nothing whatever. To this Mine own Self, the Omnipotent, the Omniscient, the All-Wise, will testify.[259]

Bahá'u'lláh

The time to choose the course of my spiritual destiny is now.

Seek the Lord while he may be found; call on him while he is near.   Isaiah 55:6

Therefore let everyone...pray to You while You may be found; surely when the mighty waters rise, they will not reach Him.   Psalms 32:4-6

In my life God comes first, before my loved ones and me. My best moments are those devoted to God. Every day I will set aside at least half an hour to know God, to love Him, and to glorify Him. I will not allow worldly concerns or selfish desires take my attention away from my responsibility to God and to all humanity. I will pray for His guidance every day.

I have total control over my choices. I do not have to follow the prejudices and untested assumptions of my ancestors. Conformity is a root cause of all evil. I will not let my spiritual destiny hang either on the wheel of chance, on my birth to my parents, on public opinion, on tradition, on conformity to authority figures, or on what my friends and relatives think.

I will use no excuses to avoid my responsibility to God, to myself, and to humankind:

> I am involved in all mankind; and therefore never send to know for whom the bell tolls; it tolls for thee.   John Donne

I will set aside a little time every day to pray to God and to ask Him to guide me by the light of His knowledge.

> O God! Refresh and gladden my spirit. Purify my heart. Illumine my powers. I lay all my affairs in Thy hand. Thou art my Guide and my Refuge...
>
> O God! Thou art more friend to me than I am to myself. I dedicate myself to Thee, O Lord.[260]
>   'Abdu'l-Bahá

> Is there any Remover of difficulties save God? Say: Praised be God! He is God! All are His servants, and all abide by His bidding![261]
>   The Báb

> Show me your ways, O Lord, teach me your paths; guide me in your truth and teach me, for you are God my Savior, and my hope is in you all day long.
>
> You are God my stronghold. Why have you rejected me? Why must I go about mourning...? Send forth your light and your truth, let them guide me; let them bring me to your holy mountain, to the place where you dwell.
>   Psalms 25:4-5; 43:2-3

Thy paradise is My love
Bahá'u'lláh

Thou shalt
be called to
account for
thy deeds
Bahá'u'lláh

The best beloved of all things in
My sight is justice
Bahá'u'lláh

Do Bahá'ís Believe in Heaven and Hell?

Many people turn away from religion because of the concept of eternal burning in hell-fire. They cannot accept a God who burns His helpless creatures for ages and eons. Because so many people are affected by this concept, it is treated here in detail.

To be true to God's Word and fair to ourselves, we should not turn away from or ignore what we don't like. What we desire will not change reality. We should, rather, face the reality with full confidence and courage and without fear. Instead of ignoring this critical word or repressing it, we should investigate and understand it.

The Bahá'í perspective of hell and heaven differs sharply from traditional beliefs. Bahá'u'lláh teaches that heaven is nearness to God and hell remoteness from His presence. True happiness comes from fellowship with God, and misery from separation from His glory.

O SON OF MAN!
Sorrow not save that thou art far from Us. Rejoice not save that thou art drawing near and returning unto Us.[262]   Bahá'u'lláh

Blessed is he that draweth nigh unto Him, and woe betide them that are far away.[263]   Bahá'u'lláh

A heart devoid of love is hell on earth and points to one beyond. A man told his guest, "Our town offers many advantages. The main problem we have is with the people and the water supply." The guest replied, "That reminds me of hell. The main problem

in hell is lack of loving people and living waters."
The road to hell is paved with apathy, impurity, and
injustice and in hell with "I wish I had...Why didn't
I? Why? Why? Why?" This is what the biblical
metaphor of "insatiable worm" means.

> ...hell...where their worm does not die, and the
> fire is not quenched. Mark 9:44-48
> (For details, see *I Shall Come Again*)

People have a tendency either to dramatize the consequences of hell in fiery and fearsome terms or to
take them lightly. Both extremes are inaccurate,
unjustified, and unhealthy; the first leads to irrational
and excessive fear, the second to apathy and a lack
of concern for the consequences of one's deeds.

God sends an invitation to all people to enter paradise. Its doors are wide open, yet some people
choose actions that prevent them from entering:

> Verily, on the First Day We flung open the gates
> of Paradise unto all the peoples of the world, and
> exclaimed: "O all ye created things! Strive to gain
> admittance into Paradise, since ye have, during
> all your lives, held fast unto virtuous deeds in
> order to attain unto it." Surely all men yearn to
> enter therein, but alas, they are unable to do so by
> reason of that which their hands have wrought.[264]
> The Báb

> He who is a true believer liveth both in this world
> and in the world to come.[265] Bahá'u'lláh

Our Creator assures us that the key to the Kingdom
is ours if we but stretch out our hands. He tells us
that heaven, with all its glory and splendor, is our
home if we but seek it with our hearts and souls.

Bahá'u'lláh makes this statement about the destiny of "the infidels"—the ones who deny God's new Messengers and Redeemers:

> The souls of the infidels, however, shall—and to this I bear witness—when breathing their last be made aware of the good things that have escaped them, and shall bemoan their plight, and shall humble themselves before God. They shall continue doing so after the separation of their souls from their bodies.[266]

As the passage implies, at the very instant of death, even before the soul is separated from the body and before we have entered the next realm, all the veils of self-deception are removed from before our eyes. Suddenly, we recognize all the excuses we have used for denying God and His Messengers and for living a selfish life. The instant of "resurrection" arrives before we have fully released the cord of life.

The Báb speaks of "pangs of remorse:"

> This mortal life is sure to perish; its pleasures are bound to fade away and ere long ye shall return unto God, distressed with pangs of remorse...ye shall soon find yourselves in the presence of God and will be asked of your doings.[267]

The Báb defines both paradise and hell-fire as:

> Paradise is attainment of His good-pleasure and everlasting hell-fire His judgment through justice.[268]

Heaven and hell are not places but conditions that can exist in both this world and in the next. To be in hell-fire is to be remote from God, the Source of all joys and perfections, and to sense a burning desire to attain His Presence.

The suffering in hell comes not only from being far from God but also from being close to the ungodly:

> Paradise is decked with mystic roses, and hell hath been made to blaze with the fire of the impious.[269]   Bahá'u'lláh

Obviously there is not much joy in hell. What happens when a mass of joyless people get together? What happens when the fire of remoteness spreads from person to person? What happens when instead of saying "I am glad" people keep saying, "I wish... If only...?" In heaven there is an abundance of perfume from "mystic roses," in hell an abundance of burning desire for the joy of nearness to God. What a contrast!

Pleasing God is the master key to paradise. The following verses declare that heaven is for those who love God and please Him. How can we truly love God and please Him? By loving and obeying the One who speaks for Him. Obeying is the inevitable consequence of loving.

> As to Paradise: It is a reality and there can be no doubt about it, and now in this world it is realized through love of Me and My good-pleasure. Whosoever attaineth unto it God will aid him in this world below, and after death He will enable him to gain admittance into Paradise whose vastness is as that of heaven and earth. Therein...the day-star of the unfading beauty of his Lord will

at all times shed its radiance upon him and he will shine so brightly that no one shall bear to gaze at him. Such is the dispensation of Providence, yet the people are shut out by a grievous veil.[270]   Bahá'u'lláh

This quote equates God's love with paradise:

> **O SON OF BEING!**
> Thy paradise is My love; thy heavenly home, reunion with Me. Enter therein and tarry not.[271]
>   Bahá'u'lláh

Recently a relative of ours—a wonderful and well-educated Bahá'í—died at a young age. Soon after her death she appeared to her aunt in a dream. When her aunt asked her how everything was there, she said, "Better than we were told." Then she added, "I appear to you the way I choose." As evidence, she instantly changed the color of her dress. By saying, "Better than we were told," she was referring to Bahá'u'lláh's references to indescribable glories and beauties beyond, such as the following statements:

> Such is the station ordained for the true believer that if to an extent smaller than a needle's eye the glory of that station were to be unveiled to mankind, every beholder would be consumed away in his longing to attain it. For this reason it hath been decreed that in this earthly life the full measure of the glory of his own station should remain concealed from the eyes of such a believer.[272]

> We dare not, in this Day, lift the veil that concealeth the exalted station which every true

believer can attain, for the joy which such a revelation must provoke might well cause a few to faint away and die.[273]

Know thou, of a truth, that if the soul of man hath walked in the ways of God, it will, assuredly, return and be gathered to the glory of the Beloved. By the righteousness of God! It shall attain a station such as no pen can depict, or tongue describe. The soul that hath remained faithful to the Cause of God, and stood unwaveringly firm in His Path shall, after his ascension, be possessed of such power that all the worlds which the Almighty hath created can benefit through him.[274]

This life is a preparation for our final exams. If we wish to enter the heavenly mansions and see the banquet of the Kingdom, we must secure our permit here and now, in the days that are still ours. As Jesus declares, the doors will remain closed to latecomers and procrastinators (Matt. 25:1-13).

Our life here is like a grand piece of art. We hold a brush in our hand. We have a choice to make a masterpiece, a mediocre work, or a horrible design. Every act touches the canvas.

This world is a place of testing. The final certificate depends on the grades we earn here. Our Creator tells us how we should live, and then leaves us alone to choose the course of our destiny. Like a teacher, He leaves the responsibility for learning and applying the knowledge entirely to us.

God's great ingenuity does not lie so much in creating the universe as in designing human beings in such a way that all of them do not seek or desire all His heavenly gifts. Some take only a drop from His vast ocean of blessings, others a handful or a cup. But a few are content with nothing short of drowning themselves in His infinite, ever-flowing, ever-enchanting riches and bounties. What keeps so many content with so little is one of the greatest mysteries in the universe. "The evangelist was approaching the finale of his fiery discourse, and his voice rose as he thundered out, 'Do you want to go to Heaven? Everyone who wants to go to Heaven, stand up!' The congregation rose as one, except for Jed Hatfield, the local ne'er-do-well. For a moment, the preacher was speechless, then he demanded, 'Brother Hatfield, don't you want to go to Heaven?' Jed looked up and drawled, 'Nope. These Tennessee hills is good enough for me.'"

We can only theorize that when God made the universe, He knew that some people love to "heap up their sins to the limit" (I Thess. 2:16) to become citizens of hell, and that others love to sanctify their souls to the limit to become citizens of heaven. Since God loves all people, He made sure that both groups could satisfy their desires. Astonishing as it may seem, many do everything within their power to become qualified for hell. They miss no opportunities to receive a space for their soul in "the fire" of remoteness from joy. The highway to heaven is quite smooth: It is paved with peace, love, harmony, hope, faith, and joy. The highway to hell is quite rough: It is paved with prejudice, anger, revenge, hatred, greed, and grudges. Yet, many choose the rough road straight to the valley of death and remoteness from God.

Another potential God gave us is the ability to engage in self-deception. Without it, life would become extremely painful. Self-deception helps us conceal our true motives and extend our freedom of choice. Have you ever met anyone who believes he will go to hell? It seems everyone thinks he was made especially for heaven.

> Atheist: "Do you honestly believe that Jonah spent three days and nights in the belly of a whale?"
>
> Preacher: "I don't know, sir, but when I get to heaven I'll ask him."
>
> Atheist: "But suppose he isn't in heaven?"
>
> Preacher: "Then you ask him!"

While on earth we have two duties: first, to know, love, and glorify God; second, to prove our love and faith by good deeds, demonstrated best by serving others. We can express our deepest love for God by acknowledging His latest Redeemers, the Báb and Bahá'u'lláh. Christ said that those who denied Him denied God. Bahá'u'lláh makes the same statement. The following statement from the Báb shows the consequences of denying the Redeemer of the age:

> For if a prophet cometh to you from God and ye fail to walk in His Way, God will, thereupon, transform your light into fire. Take heed then that perchance ye may, through the grace of God and His signs, be enabled to redeem your souls.[275]

In the following passages, the Báb reveals the blessings of remaining loyal to God's covenant:

There is no paradise more wondrous for any soul than to be exposed to God's Manifestation in His Day, to hear His verses and believe in them, to attain His presence, which is naught but the presence of God, and to partake of the choice fruits of the paradise of His divine Oneness.[276]

There is no paradise...more exalted than to obey God's commandments, and there is no fire... fiercer than to transgress His laws and to oppress another soul, even to the extent of a mustard seed. On the Day of Resurrection God will, in truth, judge all men, and we all verily plead for His grace.[277]

This world, in spite of its many pains and pressures, appears enchanting and glamorous. We often become so blinded by earthly glamours that we lose sight of heavenly glories. A little spiritual wealth is worth more than all the earthly riches, yet most people worry more about earning pennies than about entering paradise. Great Messengers seek to awaken us from our illusions of attachment to this planet, to draw our attention away from passing pleasures to the splendors of heaven:

Night hath succeeded day, and day hath succeeded night, and the hours and moments of your lives have come and gone, and yet none of you hath, for one instant, consented to detach himself from that which perisheth. Bestir yourselves, that the brief moments that are still yours may not be dissipated and lost. Even as the swiftness of lightning your days shall pass, and your bodies shall be laid to rest beneath a canopy of dust.

What can ye then achieve? How can ye atone for
your past failure?[278]   Bahá'u'lláh

Life is brief but precious. We are moving with incredible speed. Our goal is to find the highway of
happiness and the exit to heaven. If we hesitate to
look and miss the chance, if we waste the precious
gift of freedom that is ours, there is no returning.
Today people are constantly rushing and running.
Do they have a destination? "The loudspeaker of the
big jet clicked on and the captain's voice announced
in a clear, even tone: 'Now there's no cause for
alarm, but we felt passengers should know that
for the last three hours we've been flying without
the benefit of radio, compass, or radar, due to the
breakdown of some key components. This means
that we are not quite sure in which direction we are
heading. You'll be glad to know, however that
we're making excellent time!'"

After passing from the earthly realm, all souls will
have a chance to advance in the heavenly realm.
Since everyone will have this chance, those farthest from God here will, in relation to others, continue to be farthest from Him. This is why hell and
heaven are said to be eternal. The consequences of
how well we do here will stay with us always.

Whatever we weave here we will wear hereafter.
After passing away, as 'Abdu'l-Bahá declares, the
soul will continue its journey forward from "the
degree of purity to which it has evolved during life
in the physical body."[279]

As the womb is the place of preparation for this
life, so is this life for the next. We should take
advantage of every opportunity to attain the greatest

growth possible. After passing away from this realm, we will not enjoy the unlimited opportunities we have had here. This world is a school. Our goal is to graduate with honor and distinction. The uniqueness and significance of this life lies in this: It determines our eternal destiny.

The conditions of the next life are beyond our comprehension. It is futile to try to know exactly what will happen or what everything will be like. Some day we will all make the journey. What we need most is patience and trust.

Our perception of the next life may be as perfect— or as imperfect—as that of children. These examples from *Angels Must Get Their Wings by Helping Little Angels Like Me* show what children think about heaven:

> "Heaven is a place where girls get turned into angels. Then God tries to do the best He can with the boys." "It's a place where you could eat all the pizza you want and never get a tummy ache." "Jesus is in heaven. He leads the prayers and I think He still likes to fiddle around and do some carpenter's stuff with his dad." "If you take a trip away from heaven, God will always leave the light on for you." "Last one to enter heaven takes out the garbage. But don't get too bummed out, because in heaven even the garbage smells real good."

In the following statement Bahá'u'lláh offers insight into the afterlife:

> Know thou of a truth that the soul, after its separation from the body, will continue to progress

until it attaineth the presence of God, in a state and condition which neither the revolution of ages and centuries, nor the changes and chances of this world, can alter. It will endure as long as the Kingdom of God, His sovereignty, His dominion and power will endure. It will manifest the signs of God and His attributes, and will reveal His loving-kindness and bounty. The movement of My Pen is stilled when it attempteth to befittingly describe the loftiness and glory of so exalted a station. The honor with which the Hand of Mercy will invest the soul is such as no tongue can adequately reveal, nor any other earthly agency describe.

Blessed is the soul which, at the hour of its separation from the body, is sanctified from the vain imaginings of the peoples of the world. Such a soul liveth and moveth in accordance with the Will of its Creator, and entereth the all-highest Paradise. The Maids of Heaven, inmates of the loftiest mansions, will circle around it, and the Prophets of God and His chosen ones will seek its companionship. With them that soul will freely converse, and will recount unto them that which it hath been made to endure in the path of God, the Lord of all worlds. If any man be told that which hath been ordained for such a soul in the worlds of God, the Lord of the throne on high and of earth below, his whole being will instantly blaze out in his great longing to attain that most exalted, that sanctified and resplendent station...

The nature of the soul after death can never be described, nor is it meet and permissible to reveal its whole character to the eyes of men. The Prophets and Messengers of God have been sent down for the sole purpose of guiding mankind to the straight Path of Truth. The purpose underlying Their revelation hath been to educate all men, that they may, at the hour of death, ascend, in the utmost purity and sanctity and with absolute detachment, to the throne of the Most High.

The light which these souls radiate is responsible for the progress of the world and the advancement of its peoples. They are like unto leaven which leaveneth the world of being, and constitute the animating force through which the arts and wonders of the world are made manifest. Through them the clouds rain their bounty upon men, and the earth bringeth forth its fruits. All things must needs have a cause, a motive power, an animating principle. These souls and symbols of detachment have provided, and will continue to provide, the supreme moving impulse in the world of being. The world beyond is as different from this world as this world is different from that of the child while still in the womb of its mother. When the soul attaineth the Presence of God, it will assume the form that best befitteth its immortality and is worthy of its celestial habitation.[280]

Thus as Bahá'u'lláh indicates:

- The human soul continues to advance after its departure from the body.

- The nature of the soul cannot be fully described.

- The purpose of God's Messengers is to prepare us spiritually not only for this life but for the next.

- The pure souls of the departed exert a profound impact on our lives.

- This world compared to the next is like the womb compared to this world.

Sacred Scriptures contain two critical words about hell. One is the "fire," the other "forever." This passage contains both these words:

> Such as have believed in God and in His signs are indeed the followers of truth and shall abide in the gardens of delight, while those who have disbelieved in God and have rejected that which He hath revealed, these shall be the inmates of the fire wherein they shall remain forever.[281]
>
> The Báb

> And the smoke of their torment goes up for ever and ever. Revelation 14:11

The word "forever" transcends human understanding, yet we should constantly ponder its meaning, for that is the most significant aspect of our nature. ***Every thoughtful person should ponder the meaning and implications of this most critical word.***

Ages and eons must pass to regain the lost blessings and honors that can be ours even in a twinkling of an eye. The possibilities for spiritual advancement here are infinite. While on the earthly plane, it takes only a moment to decide to step from the darkness of denial into the light of hope and faith. Eternal joy is only one step away from eternal grief and sorrow:

O SON OF LOVE!
Thou art but one step away from the glorious heights above and from the celestial tree of love.

Take thou one pace and with the next advance into the immortal realm and enter the pavilion of eternity. Give ear then to that which hath been revealed by the pen of glory.[282]

Every intelligent person should ask this question: Is it worth risking an eternity for a little negligence or inattention? Is it wise to ignore God's numerous warnings for trivial reasons or excuses such as: "I am too busy," "I am not interested," or "I am happy with what I have"?

It is hard to imagine an act that would require so little effort and yet offer so much reward. It is hard to think of an act that would result from so little negligence and yet lead to such dire consequences.

This prayer should ascend from our hearts to Heaven on every moment of our lives:

> All that I beg of Thee, O my God, is to enable me, ere my soul departeth from my body, to attain Thy good-pleasure, even were it granted to me for a moment tinier than the infinitesimal fraction of a mustard seed. For if it departeth while Thou art pleased with me, then I shall be free from every concern or anxiety; but if it abandoneth me while Thou art displeased with me, then, even had I wrought every good deed, none would be of any avail, and had I earned every honor and glory, none would serve to exalt me.[283]   The Báb

We often complain about adversity—poverty, pain, despair, grief, disease, unemployment, depression, failure, and loss—and do everything within our power to avoid them. Yet we seldom think of a far

greater adversity—remoteness from God for all
eternity—and do little to avoid it. This prayer from
the Báb speaks to this point:

> O my God! O my Master! I beseech Thee by
> Thy manifold bounties and by the pillars which
> sustain Thy throne of glory, to have pity on these
> lowly people who are powerless to bear the un-
> pleasant things of this fleeting life, how much
> less then can they bear Thy chastisement in the
> life to come—a chastisement which is ordained
> by Thy justice, called forth by Thy wrath and
> will continue to exist for ever.[284]

We have total control over the heaven and the hell
we create in both worlds. Love on earth leads to
splendor, glory, and peace in heaven; hate on earth
leads to sadness, grief, and pain in hell. An open
heart to God's invitation on earth leads to an open
gate to His heavenly banquet. A closed heart to
God's invitation on earth leads to a closed gate to
His heavenly banquet.

The greatest and most splendid crown of honor and
glory a human being can ever acquire is recognizing
the Redeemer of the age, loving Him, and living by
His law. At death, each soul carries this precious
crown from here to hereafter. To live and have an
opportunity but fail to gain this glorious crown is
a loss unimaginable. It is infinitely greater than all
the losses, failures, and tragedies a human being
can encounter over a lifetime. For no matter how
severe the pains, they will pass away; but the pain
of denying the greatest gift that God gives to human
beings—His supreme Messengers and Redeemers—
will endure for all eternity.

Better is guidance for him who is guided than all the things that exist on earth, for by reason of this guidance he will, after his death, gain admittance into Paradise...Hence God desireth that all men should be guided aright...However, such as are conceited will not suffer themselves to be guided. They will be debarred from the Truth, some by reason of their learning, others on account of their glory and power, and still others due to reasons of their own, none of which shall be of any avail at the hour of death.[285]   The Báb

The following passage from the Gospel shows that "eternal life" is bestowed on those who recognize God and His supreme Messenger Jesus Christ:

Now this is eternal life: that they may know you, the only true God, and Jesus Christ, whom you have sent.   John 17:3

Honoring the One God sends is absolutely essential:

He who does not honor the Son does not honor the Father, who sent him.   Christ (John 5:23)

The same principle holds true today. The Spirit is the same, only the name has changed. To gain eternal life, we must acknowledge the Báb and Bahá'u'lláh, who are sent for our time. What is the opposite of eternal life? It is spiritual "death." In God's sight, anyone who rejects His Redeemer has rejected Him and is counted as spiritually dead. For some people this awareness may be too painful, but it is everyone's right and responsibility to know.

Here are some Bahá'í prayers for the departed:

O my God! O Thou forgiver of sins, bestower of gifts, dispeller of afflictions!

Verily, I beseech Thee to forgive the sins of such as have abandoned the physical garment and have ascended to the spiritual world.

O my Lord! Purify them from trespasses, dispel their sorrows, and change their darkness into light. Cause them to enter the garden of happiness, cleanse them with the most pure water, and grant them to behold Thy splendors on the loftiest mount.[286]   'Abdu'l-Bahá

O my God! O my God! Verily Thy servant, humble before the majesty of Thy divine supremacy, lowly at the door of Thy oneness, hath believed in Thee and in Thy verses, hath testified to Thy word, hath been enkindled with the fire of Thy love, hath been immersed in the depths of the ocean of Thy knowledge, hath been attracted by Thy breezes, hath relied upon Thee, hath turned his face to Thee, hath offered his supplications to Thee, and hath been assured of Thy pardon and forgiveness. He hath abandoned this mortal life and hath flown to the kingdom of immortality, yearning for the favor of meeting Thee.

O Lord, glorify his station, shelter him under the pavilion of Thy supreme mercy, cause him to enter Thy glorious paradise, and perpetuate his existence in Thine exalted rose garden, that he may plunge into the sea of light in the world of mysteries.

Verily, Thou art the Generous, the Powerful, the Forgiver and the Bestower.[287]   'Abdu'l-Bahá

What Are the Two Levels of Knowledge?

As powerful as ignorance is, it has an equally powerful antidote: knowledge.

> In truth, knowledge is a veritable treasure for man, and a source of glory, of bounty, of joy, of exaltation, of cheer and gladness unto him.[288]
>
> Bahá'u'lláh

> The light of the people of the world is their knowledge and utterance...[289]   The Báb

Knowledge here does not refer to the acquisition of facts, but to the *awareness of truth*. Knowledge without love for truth is only thin air:

> Knowledge puffs up, but love builds up.
>
> I Corinthians 8:1

The two most significant levels of awareness are *knowing*, and *seeing*.

> I have *heard* of You by the hearing of the ear, but now my eyes *see* You.   Job 42:5

Think of your heart as iron and of truth as acid. Can any interaction take place between the two elements as long as they are kept apart? The same principle applies to knowing. Unless knowledge reaches the stage of "insight," no interaction can ensue. Or think of knowledge as the sun. Can simply knowing about the sun change your health or your life? No, only when you bask in its light can you be influenced by its powers. Everyone has the potential not only to know God but to see Him, with his or her heart and soul.

Blessed are the pure in heart, for they shall see God.
Christ (Matt. 5:8)

What happens when the heart is blinded? It turns into a veil.

I dealt with them [Israelites] according to their uncleanness and their offenses, and *hid My Face from them*.
Ezekiel 39:24

The main reason religion has little impact on people's lives is that it exists mostly in the stage of knowing. It is rooted in the mind, but not the heart.

Every poll taken in recent years shows that more than 90 percent of Americans believe in God. A recent Gallup poll indicates that "96 percent of Americans believe in God...90 percent believe in heaven...79 percent believe in miracles...and 72 percent believe in angels." And yet crime, violence, abuse, and fraud are rampant.

The most essential knowledge is from and about God. Without the light of that knowledge, which comes through His Messengers, the soul remains in total darkness:

I am the light of the world.
Christ (John 9:5)

God hath manifested Me with a light that hath encompassed all that are in the heavens and all that are on earth.[290]
Bahá'u'lláh

The signs and tokens of the Truth shine even as the midday sun, and yet the people are wandering, aimlessly and perplexedly, in the wilderness of ignorance and folly.[291]
Bahá'u'lláh

The first requirement for living in peace and joy is to decipher the mystery of God—to know Him as intimately as possible. Once that is accomplished, everything else will take care of itself. Only the knowledge of God can give meaning and purpose to our lives.

> The beginning of all things is the knowledge of God...[292]   Bahá'u'lláh

> True knowledge, therefore, is the knowledge of God, and this is none other than the recognition of His Manifestation in each Dispensation.[293]
>   The Báb

> The source of all learning is the knowledge of God, exalted be His glory, and this cannot be attained save though the knowledge of His Divine Manifestation.[294]   Bahá'u'lláh

> "Knowledge is a light which God casteth into the heart of whomsoever He willeth." It is this kind of knowledge which is and hath ever been praiseworthy, and not the limited knowledge that hath sprung forth from veiled and obscured minds.[295]
>   Bahá'u'lláh

Knowledge of God reaches and interacts only with pure hearts, just as the rays of the sun glow with full glory and power only in clean mirrors.

As ignorance is the source and essence of all vices, so are knowledge and love for truth the sources and essence of all virtues:

> The essence of all that We have revealed for thee is Justice, is for man to free himself from idle fancy and imitation, discern with the eye of

oneness His glorious handiwork, and look into all
things with a searching eye.[296]   Bahá'u'lláh

In the preceding statement, Bahá'u'lláh singles out
five qualities:

- Justice
- Freedom from idle fancy, illusions, or myths
- Freedom from blind conformity and imitation
- The ability to look into everything with a searching eye
- The ability to discern with the eye of oneness, to see the "big picture," as God does

Only a small minority can fulfill all these requirements. Once again we can see why, throughout all ages, truth has been suppressed and resisted. No wonder so many remain with the religion of their ancestors. If they met all the preceding requirements, they would have discovered the essential oneness of all great faiths. They would have lived in peace and harmony. They would have recognized the truth of *One God, Many Faiths; One Garden, Many Flowers.*

What Are the Traits of a True Seeker?

Everything revolves around this question: How ready and receptive is your heart to new knowledge, beliefs, and attitudes? Is your heart thirsty for truth? Bahá'u'lláh teaches that if someone is not thirsty for living waters, he should not be offered a cup:

O SON OF DUST!

The wise are they that speak not unless they obtain a hearing, even as the cup-bearer, who proffereth not his cup till he findeth a seeker, and the lover who crieth not out from the depths of his heart until he gazeth upon the beauty of his beloved. Wherefore sow the seeds of wisdom and knowledge in the pure soil of the heart, and keep them hidden, till the hyacinths of divine wisdom spring from the heart and not from mire and clay.[297]

Christ used a beautiful parable to show the great variety of hearts people have. First, He spoke about the fulfillment of Isaiah's prophecy concerning those who would deny their Messiah:

> Though seeing, they do not see; though hearing, they do not hear or understand. In them is fulfilled the prophecy of Isaiah: "You will be ever hearing but never understanding; you will be ever seeing but never perceiving. For this people's heart has become calloused; they hardly hear with their ears, and they have closed their eyes. Otherwise they might see with their eyes, hear with their ears, understand with their hearts and turn, and I would heal them."   Matthew 13:13-15

Then He referred to a few disciples who were exceptions:

> But blessed are your eyes because they see, and your ears because they hear.   Matthew 13:16

After complimenting His dear disciples, Jesus revealed the parable of the sower:

> Listen then to what the parable of the sower means: When anyone hears the message about

the kingdom and does not understand it, the evil one comes and snatches away what was sown in his heart. This is the seed sown along the path. The one who received the seed that fell on rocky places is the man who hears the word and at once receives it with joy. But since he has no root, he lasts only a short time. When trouble or persecution comes because of the word, he quickly falls away. The one who received the seed that fell among the thorns is the man who hears the word, but the worries of this life and the deceitfulness of wealth choke it, making it unfruitful. But the one who received the seed that fell on good soil is the man who hears the word and understands it. He produces a crop, yielding a hundred, sixty or thirty times what was sown. Matthew 13:18-23

The Báb compares a person without spiritual capacity to a stone, and the one with capacity to a mirror:

The One true God may be compared unto the sun and the believer unto a mirror. No sooner is the mirror placed before the sun than it reflects its light. The unbeliever may be likened unto a stone. No matter how long it is exposed to the sunshine, it cannot reflect the sun.[298]

'Abdu'l-Bahá presents a similar analogy to portray the same principle:

Behold how the sun shines upon all creation, but only surfaces that are pure and polished can reflect its glory and light...Green and living trees can absorb the bounty of the sun; dead roots and withered branches are destroyed by it. Therefore, man must seek capacity and develop readiness.[299]

Bahá'u'lláh begins His *Book of Certitude*, which pertains to the proofs of His divine Mission, with these verses:

> No man shall attain the shores of the ocean of true understanding except he be detached from all that is in heaven and on earth. Sanctify your souls, O ye peoples of the world, that haply ye may attain that station which God hath destined for you...[300]

In this statement, Bahá'u'lláh considers two conditions essential for finding the truth:

- ***detachment***
- ***sanctity***

What is detachment? Life on earth can be compared to a plane ride, and God to the solid ground that supports and sustains our souls. Our goal is to jump out of the plane, which is our ego, and away from the clouds, which are the illusions that surround us.

Detachment means separating yourself temporarily from whatever you have learned. It means starting your spiritual journey with no preconceived notions. It means stepping out of your plane with no strings attached, simply for the sake of beholding wonders you have never seen before. Of course, when you jump, you carry a parachute, which at the right moment opens to protect you and to allow you to descend gracefully and confidently. The parachute is the potential—the pure mind and the pure heart—that God placed in your soul to protect you from self-destruction. If you trust Him and put everything in His hand, he will open your parachute at the right moment. He will help you open your mind and soul to the splendors of His light. What will happen if you jump with a cord attached to you and to the plane? You will dangle dangerously.

Thus, to find the truth, you must put everything aside— everything you have learned from your parents, your pastor, your priest, or any other "authority figure." If you begin your journey with any strings attached, you will be dragged, dangling, behind the plane.

The second condition Bahá'u'lláh considers essential for finding the truth is sanctity. Attachment originates mostly in the emotions, especially the fear of losing something precious; sanctity pertains mostly to the purity of the soul.

Think of your soul as a sheet of paper. Can anyone write a clear message on a cluttered page? The more cluttered the page, the harder it is to write. God is always looking for a blank space on our soul to write special messages, such as hope and happiness. He constantly declares that He loves us. That is why He made us. He created the universe for our sake and provided for us every heavenly gift imaginable. He sent His most glorious creations, His Messengers of hope and peace, and allowed them to suffer for our sake. He gave us every potential, every celestial gift from His heavenly treasures. He did not withhold anything from us. We manifest His beauty and grandeur. What more can we expect? Our only duty in return for all these blessings is to leave a little blank space for Him, so that He can keep writing His special messages of love for us.

What will happen if our souls are cluttered with worldliness? How can God find space to write?

What will happen if our souls are cluttered with self-satisfaction, greed, selfishness, pride, pretension, self-deception, prejudice, and plausible excuses? What will happen if a person writes messages like these:

- O God, I love you, but I am really too busy! (A common and seemingly innocent excuse for putting one's immediate self-interest above one's duty to God.)

- O God, I love you, but investigating the news of the Advent of the One you have promised is not my job. There are thousands of other people who know the Scripture better than I do. I depend on them. If there is any "good news," they will tell me. (Another unacceptable excuse.)

- O God, I love you, but I am afraid! How do I know I will not be deceived? (Another seemingly innocent excuse for avoiding personal responsibility.)

We can continue endlessly finding a hundred other excuses people give for avoiding their responsibility to God, to themselves, and to society. The result is this: We keep the page so full, make it so cluttered with personal messages and excuses, there is no room for God's angels to write.

Human beings are experts at blaming others and finding excuses. A little girl asked a famous musician for his autograph. "Sorry my hand is too tired from playing." he claimed. "My hands are even more tired from applauding!" she responded.

God sends us many clues and gives us many signs to help us to find Him and follow Him. We must become sensitive to these clues and discover their inner meanings. It is said that nothing happens by coincidence, that there is a reason for everything. We can discover the reasons only if we attune our souls to the heavenly music. God constantly sends us messages, but we are too busy to listen. He offers us many opportunities that we ignore.

We must pray constantly to become worthy of the gifts of God. Seeing Him with our hearts and souls is the most precious of all gifts. It does not come by force, but by capacity. We must pray for a greater capacity. A little girl loved maple syrup and often dipped her finger into the big barrel. One day, she fell in and, as she was sinking, she prayed, "O Lord, make me equal to the opportunity!" That should be our daily prayer. The ocean of God's gifts and blessings is endless. We all have a chance to immerse our souls in the Word of God:

> Immerse yourselves in the ocean of My words, that ye may unravel its secrets, and discover all the pearls of wisdom that lie hid in its depths.[301]
>
> Bahá'u'lláh

We must constantly polish our hearts to make them as pure as glass, so that they may absorb the light. God does not wish to live in a dirty house. Would you? Would you touch your pure and precious garment with dirty hands?

> **O SON OF BEING!**
> Thy heart is My home; sanctify it for My descent. Thy spirit is My place of revelation; cleanse it for My manifestation.[302]
>
> Bahá'u'lláh

O WEED THAT SPRINGETH OUT OF DUST!
Wherefore have not these soiled hands of thine touched first thine own garment, and why with thine heart defiled with desire and passion dost thou seek to commune with Me and to enter My sacred realm? Far, far are ye from that which ye desire.[303]   Bahá'u'lláh

This life is a test. What is the purpose of a test? To reveal what lies hidden. Every opportunity, every challenge reveals our inner motives; it shows whether we are fearful or bold, narrow-minded or broad-minded, bound by tradition or by truth, by self-interest or by common-interest.

> In dealing with men it is God's purpose to test them and to see what they truly are.
>
> Ecclesiastes 3:18

The grading of all the tests is done at the end of this life, which is the beginning of the next. That is the most awesome scene in the eternal destiny of every human being. No one can escape it. At that point we will receive our final evaluations. We will be told how we have scored.

The news of the coming of great Messengers presents the most challenging and decisive test for human beings. Some people hear the news and ignore it; others scan it briefly and stop; some investigate it all their lives but never make a commitment; others accept it but do little to promote it; some oppose it; and others embrace it and promote it with all their hearts and souls.

The test of recognizing God's Messengers and Redeemers is mostly spiritual; it pertains to the heart and soul. If people acted according to reason, proof, and evidence, the whole world would be Bahá'ís. For, as we noted, the rational evidence for the Bahá'í Faith is overwhelming. But unless the hearts are ready and receptive, no amount of evidence can make any difference.

To pass a test, the individual must meet certain requirements, must make certain preparations. Unless those requirements are met, the individual cannot succeed. How can a seeker pass his or her tests? What are the traits of a true seeker? Are you willing to test yourself? It is wise to look at your soul objectively and without fear. Your whole destiny depends on your courage and desire to know yourself. The following is a test. The left column lists the standards by which you can judge yourself; it shows the traits of a true seeker. The right column offers you an opportunity to rate yourself. In relation to each trait listed, give yourself a rating from 1 to 5: 1 indicates that you judge yourself to be farthest away from the true seeker; 5 shows you are closest.

A true seeker:	*Rate yourself:*

- Has a deep desire to find the truth and pursues it with unwavering resolve. Searches for truth like the one who has lost a jewel.

Farthest away from a true seeker / Closest to a true seeker
1 2 3 4 5

- Tests everything *for himself*, and does not depend on others—parents, peers, or pastors—to judge or decide. Refuses to seek safety in tradition or popularity.

1 2 3 4 5

A true seeker:

Rate yourself:

| | Farthest away from the true seeker | | Closest to the true seeker |

- Selfish interests do not stand in his way: "How will my friends react?" "What will my parents say?" Such questions may enter his mind, but they do not affect his judgment.

1 2 3 4 5

- Erases from his mind all preconceived notions. Like a member of a jury, he begins with a clear slate. (Some people even allow a new name to affect their judgment. They refuse to study the Bahá'í Faith because, they say, it "sounds" strange!) A true seeker does not, as 'Abdu'l-Bahá states, "while loving and clinging to one form of religion, permit himself to detest all others."[304]

1 2 3 4 5

- Is sincere and does not argue merely to win a point.

1 2 3 4 5

- Is patient and persistent, and willingly invests ample time and effort to discover his heart's desire.

1 2 3 4 5

- Has a good heart, free from deception, hypocrisy, and pretension.

1 2 3 4 5

- Is humble enough to say, "I don't know," and confident enough to say, "I can find out."

1 2 3 4 5

- Trusts God and prays constantly with all his heart and soul for His help.

1 2 3 4 5

A true seeker:

- Does not allow an emotional attachment to a given name to prevent him from accepting and loving a new name.

Rate yourself:

Farthest away from the true seeker			Closest to the true seeker	
1	2	3	4	5

If you give yourself 4 and 5 in all categories, you may be free from major emotional-spiritual obstacles and disabilities. Scores of 1 and 2 show serious disabilities, even if it is in only one of the ten categories listed. Please review the discussion on the role of "the weakest critical link" in human lives in Volume II, *Heaven's Most Glorious Gift.* Remember what happened to the spacecraft *Challenger* because of one critical flaw in its complex system. The same can happen to human beings. One critical flaw in your soul may hold you back from the light of truth. Remember also the analogy used by Bahá'u'lláh that a veil as small as an eyelid conceals the sun.

A score of 3 puts you in a state of conflict. You will be pulled by two opposite forces. In this case, as a rule, your conservative, safety-seeking nature will overcome your adventurous side. This is the way most people behave; they prefer their comfort zones. Even a single score of 3 can be a definite disadvantage.

As you can see, the spiritual path for most people is full of pitfalls and obstacles. To make the journey from your comfort zone through the steep valleys and the high mountains, you will need 4s and 5s in all ten categories. If you are a religious leader, in addition to facing all these challenges, you must contemplate and cope with the loss of the source of your livelihood. This requires much courage and detachment. Of course, the greater the sacrifice, the greater your reward.

If you lack, or fail to acquire, any of these ten virtues, you may be unable to discern the truth. Even a small patch of clouds can conceal the blazing splendor of the sun. Discovering and overcoming your special handicaps or "weakest critical links" is the first step in the search for truth. Taking this first step is perhaps the most challenging task. It requires absolute open-mindedness and dedication.

The fact that all the divine Messengers have been rejected by the overwhelming majority of people in their age is the best evidence of how difficult and vital it is to practice an "independent search for the truth."

Perhaps the weakest critical link in human beings is a failure to see and recognize one's own weaknesses. Do you ever recall meeting someone who said, "I am fanatical, egotistical, prejudiced, unloving, unjust, closed-minded, unwise, and irresponsible"?

One of the many traits that can prevent us from seeing the truth is pride. Few things in life are as difficult to detect as pride in one's ego. It is as natural as breathing, and as toxic and invisible as radiation. Would you like to be tested? Consider these verses addressed to a people who lived long ago:

> Woe to you...you hypocrites! You build tombs for the prophets and decorate the graves for the righteous. And you say, "If we had lived in the days of our forefathers, we would not have taken

part with them in shedding the blood of the
prophets."   Christ (Matt. 23:29-30)

Suppose you lived in 27 A. D. and were a neighbor
of Annas and Caiaphas, the two most prominent
religious leaders among the Jews at the time of
Jesus. As you may know, they both insisted that
Christ be crucified. What would be the chances that
you, their neighbor, would have opposed their verdict? If you genuinely believe that you would have
gone along with your distinguished neighbors as
well as the masses of people, spiritually you are in
good shape, relatively free from pride. Remember
that the odds against Christ were so high that
even His handful of beloved and distinguished
disciples failed to defend Him.

Once again, suppose you lived at the time of Noah.
What would be your chances of denying Him? We
could repeat this question many times. Each time
you would say, "Very likely, I would have been
among the masses of deniers of truth." If that is
quite likely, isn't it also quite likely that you may
be in the same position? It should actually be easier
for you to say "yes," because you can readily see
a recurring and consistent record of denial at the
dawn of the Advent of every divine Messenger.

The acknowledgment—that you would have been
quite likely among the deniers—will move you to
cleanse your soul from every lingering traces of ego,
from any inclination to say, "I know I am right. If
it had happened, I would have known it." This
acknowledgment may cause you to think deeply, to
ponder, even to feel anxious or to sense a little

fear. Such fear or anxiety is perfectly healthy. It will cause you to act. It will protect you from spiritual starvation, just as fear of physical death protects you from drunken driving.

Please try this process of questioning "What would be the chances..." on a few people you know: your friends, relatives, even your rabbi, pastor, or priest. Find out if they are willing to see themselves among the deniers. Then tell them about the Báb and Bahá'u'lláh, and see if they suddenly make an exception, such as "No, this time it is different! I am pretty sure this could not have happened without my knowledge!" Please ponder this verse:

> There is a way that seems right to a man, but in the end it leads to [spiritual] death. Proverbs 14:12

Which way leads to death?

It is the easy way.

It is ignoring an invitation to investigate.

It is asking someone else to tell you the right way.

It is saying, "One billion people cannot be wrong."

It is thinking, "I am too busy."

It is failing to pray for guidance.

It is being afraid.

It is procrastinating.

It is wondering what others will say.

It is being attached to a well-established name.

The right way is usually narrow and uphill—straight to God. It is paved with humility, courage, detachment, trust, thirst for truth, and self-sacrifice. The wrong way is usually wide and downhill—straight away from God. It is paved with pride, complacency, apathy, and immediate self-interests.

I have a close friend who is a retired pastor. It is hard to find a person more caring, more honest, more charitable, more hard-working, and more friendly. He is as good as a human being can be. He even spent a few days in prison for demonstrating against a war he believed was unjust. I thought he would be the best candidate for a book on the Bahá'í Faith. Therefore, I gave him a copy of *I Shall Come Again*, a 500-page volume that presents biblical prophecies about the Advents of the Báb and Bahá'u'lláh. In response to my invitation to read the book, he said, "I read a lot of books. I can finish it in a week or two." He made that statement two years ago. Since then, I have seen him several times. Each time, I have asked him if he has read the book, and each time he has presented a new alibi. The last time I asked him, he showed both embarrassment and annoyance.

All his life he has been exposed to the glorious hope of the Second Coming, and talked about it in his church. Now that he has in his hands a book that presents far more evidence on the Second Advent than he could ever find on the First, he procrastinates, he ignores his most glorious hope! He knows that because of his position, he has a special responsibility to investigate the news of the coming of his Master, yet he fails to heed the warnings and seek the blessings.

My pastor friend knows he is a wonderful person. Because of his confidence in his own goodness, he doesn't dream that he may even be denying the One he has worshiped all his life. He may not realize that even the most wonderful people can fail. Both the laws of the physical and spiritual worlds are such that sometimes a little caution may result in gigantic gains. An inexpensive fire alarm can save countless lives. A failure as innocent as remaining silent, as simple as ignoring a warning can be disastrous. Silence is not always innocent. As it is said, all that evil requires to triumph is for good people to do nothing.

If Annas and Caiaphas had followed Christ, it is quite likely that He would not have been crucified. Without question, there were thousands of wonderful people among the Jews who ignored Christ's invitation. Remember that before becoming a Christian, St. Paul was a wonderful, dedicated Jew. He was as firm in his beliefs as my pastor friend. Yet he suffered from this critical weakness: he was narrow-minded. If God had not intervened, he would have continued to persecute the Christians.

There are millions of wonderful Christians living today. I have the honor of knowing many of them. Without their love and dedication, our planet would become a gloomy place. They are, indeed, the salt of the earth. Yet many of them suffer from this critical weakness: They simply assume that if Christ had come, they would have known it. That was the assumption Paul made. He was expecting a powerful King—a Messiah who would subdue the forces of darkness just as Christians expect today.

That one seemingly innocent assumption that "If Christ comes I will know" kills all curiosity and creates complacency, a weakness Jesus condemned most severely in the Book of Revelation. But none of those millions of wonderful, but slumbering people, thinks that those passages about complacency may refer to him. When he does, he awakens and begins to investigate. Once again we end where we started: It is extremely difficult to see the traces of pride, fear, or complacency in one's ego. A sure remedy is an absolute and unconditional humility.

If you are open-minded, you will attain the greatest good. For the mind is the first gate to wisdom, truth, and happiness. After the mind has done its work, the heart must prepare a place to welcome the truth with warmth and joy.

Bahá'u'lláh teaches that the seeker of truth must pray constantly and sincerely for divine guidance. This prophecy is about us, the people of this age:

> For many are invited, but few are chosen.
>
> Christ (Matt. 22:14)

Both the preceding and the following verses indicate that the choice is mutual: As we choose God, so does God choose us.

> No one can come to Me unless the Father has enabled him.
>
> Christ (John 6:65)

Entering God's Kingdom requires certain qualifications. When we sanctify our souls and humble our hearts, then God says, "You are worthy of my grace." That is why praying is so essential. By praying, we ask God to make us receptive to His call and deserving of the honor of entering His Kingdom and of meeting Him.

Praying is a connecting link by which God's grace can reach us. Bahá'u'lláh declares that the grace of God is sufficient, but it must first be activated by some means:

> For results depend upon means, and the grace of God shall be all-sufficient unto you.[305]

We should recognize that we were made for a purpose much greater than eating, drinking, marrying, and being merry. Only by seeking the knowledge of God, as revealed through His latest Redeemer, can we attain the purpose for which we were created. If we reject that knowledge, He will reject us.

> Because thou hath rejected knowledge, I will also reject thee...   Hosea 4:6

I began my spiritual adventures many years ago. My most intensive search began at age 27. At that point, I decided to read one book each week until I came to a definitive conclusion about the Báb and Bahá'u'lláh. Within two years, I had read about 100 Bahá'í books. I read everything I could find. Some people have a hard time finishing even a book like this one. They underestimate the grave consequences of failing to acquire spiritual knowledge.

These principles bind us to our Creator:

- *freedom*   • *responsibility*
- *knowledge*   • *reward and punishment*

Because you are fortunate to have received the gift of the knowledge of Bahá'u'lláh, you are responsible to do everything within your power to help the seed of your knowledge to grow, and to bear celestial fruits for your soul. Your eternal destiny depends on it. It is far better for a person not to know than to know but take no action. Isn't that the way we treat our children? Do we not consider them responsible only *after* we have told them the rules, only *after* we have given them the gift of knowledge of right and wrong?

> From anyone who has been given much, much will be demanded; and from the one who has been entrusted with much, much more will be asked. Luke 12:48

The world is in a desperate shape. Many unskilled doctors are offering instant remedies, but the patient is getting sicker. We can rectify the prevailing defective world order quickly and painlessly by accepting and applying God's remedy; or we can prolong our suffering by refusing to apply the remedy:

> George was having trouble with a toothache, so he decided to visit the dentist.
>
> "What do you charge for extracting a tooth?" George asked.
>
> "Fifty dollars," replied the dentist.
>
> "Fifty dollars for only ten minutes' work?" exclaimed George.
>
> "Well," replied the dentist, "if you wish, I can extract it very slowly."

This volume, *One God, Many Faiths; One Garden, Many Flowers* and its sequel *Heaven's Most Glorious Gift*, do not tell the full story of this supreme Revelation. They are mainly a call, an eye-opener.

Their goal is to awaken you to the dawning of this great day of the Lord:

Happy the man who stays awake...
Christ (Rev. 16:15)

I beseech God, exalted be His glory, that He may graciously awaken the peoples of the earth...[306]
Bahá'u'lláh

Be on guard! Be alert...keep watch...don't let him find you sleeping.   Christ (Mark 13:33-37)

As 'Abdu'l-Bahá states, to attain and accomplish a goal, three conditions must be met:

- *knowing*
- *deciding*
- *acting*

You have met all three conditions *on a small scale*. You heard about the Bahá'í Faith, you decided to investigate it, and you acted on your decision. Now you need to continue your investigation until you have reached *the point of certainty*. That point comes when your knowledge turns into vision, when you move from the stage of "knowing" to the stage of "seeing."

Once Jesus gave this standard as a way of separating truth from falsehood:

If a man chooses to do God's will, he will find out whether my teaching comes from God or whether I speak on my own.   Christ (John 7:17)

The same rule applies to Bahá'u'lláh's teachings. What is God's will? It is to use *His* standards, not our own. Two of the most essential standards our Creator asks us to use are these:

- *good fruits*
- *fulfillment of prophecies*

Bahá'u'lláh fulfills both of these standards. He fulfills the second one on a scale that has never been seen before. A list of references, which covers both fruits and prophecies, is offered at the end of this book.

What Is the Illusion of Waiting and Wishing?

Bahá'u'lláh speaks again and again of *fancies*, *illusions*, and *idle imaginings* that dominate our lives.

O SON OF MAN!
Many a day hath passed over thee whilst thou hast busied thyself with thy *fancies and idle imaginings*. How long art thou to slumber on thy bed? Lift up thy head from slumber, for the Sun hath risen to the zenith, haply it may shine upon thee with the light of beauty [emphasis added].[307]

An illusion is a false assumption that we accept as true and then give it full power and authority to direct the course of our lives and destinies. Among the countless illusions human beings cherish is that of *waiting and wishing*. What are they waiting for? Here are just a few examples from a long list prepared by an author:

- Inspiration
- Permission
- Reassurance
- More time
- A significant relationship
- A disaster
- Time to almost run out

- An obvious scapegoat
- The kids to leave home
- The lion to lie down with the lamb
- A better time
- A more favorable horoscope
- An absence of risk
- Someone to discover me
- More adequate safeguards
- My love to rekindle
- My ego to improve
- My self-esteem to be restored
- Someone to be watching me
- A clearly written set of instructions
- The pot to boil
- Spring
- Various aches and pains to subside
- Shorter lincs at the bank
- Someone else to screw up
- The next time around
- You to stand out of my light
- California to fall into the ocean
- My grandfather's estate to be settled
- A cue card
- You to go first
- A signal from Heaven[308]

An enchanting illusion popular among many believers is that if they wait long enough, they will be suddenly raptured or raised to the heavens on high. They are waiting for an angel to come to their place of residence, greet them, embrace them, lift them by their hands, lead them high into the heavens, and then put them with all their loved ones in the gardens of peace and gladness—where they will live forevermore, where they can look down on all the sinners and their doubting friends on earth and say, "I told you so!" The problem is this: Many of those who cherish and enjoy such fancies are so intensely gripped by fear of being deceived that they do not even dare to take their hands out of their pockets, lest they will be picked by the wrong angel! They are so careful, they do not even look heavenward for fear of attracting a deceiving angel! They feel the safest place is the comfort zone of their own denomination. They are so conservative, they even insure their hats!

As people fear the loss of their possessions, so do they fear the loss of their faith. Anyone with a different belief system is considered a potential thief. What is the best protection against a thief? A security system and a locked house. What is the best protection against the loss of faith? Systematic avoidance, ignorance, and a closed mind.

Studies indicate that those who face a fatal disease or approach old age often have this regret: I wish I had been more daring; I wish I had been more adventurous. Consider the following passage from the memoirs of an old person on the verge of passing from this life:

- I've been one of those people who never go anywhere without a thermometer, a hot-water bottle, a raincoat, and a parachute.
- If I had my life to live over, I would start barefoot earlier in the spring and stay that way later in the fall.
- I'd dare to make more mistakes next time.
- I would take more chances.
- I would travel lighter next time.

- I would climb more mountains and swim more rivers.
- I would go to more dances.
- I would ride more merry-go-rounds.
- I would pick more daisies.[309]

What does the illusion of waiting and wishing teach us? It teaches us that the world does not wait for anyone; that apathy, inaction, and fear stifle the human spirit; that courage and a sense of adventure are the attributes of the faithful; that we must cherish the honor of choosing our everlasting destiny before we have lost that chance. Simply waiting and wishing for a miracle will not lead us to the haven of hope and peace. As a rule, it leads us to the depths of despair. The parable of the talent uttered by Jesus (Matt. 25:14-30) testifies to the truth of this principle.

The powers and intensity of illusions and fancies in human life are incredible. They are so vast and fascinating that they deserve an entire volume.

Why Do People Accept the Bahá'í Faith?

In spite of many obstacles, according to *Britannica Book of the Year*, the Bahá'í Faith is the second most widely spread religion in the world. (Christianity is the first.) Further, the rate of its spread has been accelerating from its very beginning. The light of Bahá'u'lláh is so dazzling that it attracts enlightened believers and seekers from all segments of society, and from all religions and cultures. These are some of the reasons why so many people have turned to the Bahá'í Faith as the fulfillment of the prophecies of all sacred Scriptures:

- They find that the Bahá'í Faith crowns their lives with hope and a glowing vision for their own futures and for the world. They gain a spiritual and eternal purpose.

- They find the Bahá'í Faith to be the fulfillment of all prophecies and promises made in their sacred Scriptures.

- They find a religion they can practice. They see harmony between their beliefs and their actions.

- They discover that the Bahá'í Faith is built on enlightened faith, not on dogmatism.

- They see harmony between their religious beliefs and scientific knowledge.

- They learn that God has been loyal to His promises and has not abandoned humanity.

- They find a religion that strengthens their family relations and provides clear moral standards for their children and youth.

- They find satisfactory answers to their unresolved questions, for the Bahá'í Faith offers a rational approach to religion.

- They learn they can do something for the world, instead of just talking about its problems.

- Because of the spiritual strength they gain, they experience fewer conflicts.

- They gain a sense of peace and joy that they have not known before.

- They find a community that is diverse yet unified.

- They discover dedicated and trustworthy friends who practice high ethical standards.
- They find that their love for God and human-kind grows stronger.

Many people search ardently for happiness. They look everywhere except where it lies in abundance. There are millions of Bahá'ís who will admit to having been quite skeptical about most or all of the benefits listed here. They will also acknowledge that, to their surprise, their skepticism faded when they saw Bahá'ís living the Bahá'í life.

Observing how the followers of a faith live is the ultimate test of that faith. The people—their ideals and their actions—are the fruits of the religion they follow.

> By their fruits you will recognize them. Do people pick grapes from thornbushes, or figs from thistles? Likewise every good tree bears good fruit, but a bad tree bears bad fruit. A good tree cannot bear bad fruit, and a bad tree cannot bear good fruit.   Christ (Matt. 7:16-19)

St. Paul describes the fruits of the Spirit of God:

> But the fruit of the Spirit is love, joy, peace, patience, kindness, goodness, faithfulness, gentle-ness and self-control.   Galatians 5:22-23

Bahá'u'lláh claims to be the Spirit sent by God. He manifests all those virtues to perfection. In His vineyard, good fruits grow in abundance.

Here is a small basketful from the vast vineyard of Bahá'í sacred Scriptures:

O peoples of the world! Forsake all evil, hold fast that which is good. Strive to be shining examples unto all mankind, and true reminders of the virtues of God amidst men. He that riseth to serve My Cause should manifest My wisdom, and bend every effort to banish ignorance from the earth. Be united in counsel, be one in thought. Let each morn be better than its eve and each morrow richer than its yesterday. Man's merit lieth in service and virtue and not in the pageantry of wealth and riches. Take heed that your words be purged from idle fancies and worldly desires and your deeds be cleansed from craftiness and suspicion. Dissipate not the wealth of your precious lives in the pursuit of evil and corrupt affection, nor let your endeavors be spent in promoting your personal interest. Be generous in your days of plenty, and be patient in the hour of loss. Adversity is followed by success and rejoicings follow woe. Guard against idleness and sloth, and cling unto that which profiteth mankind, whether young or old, whether high or low. Beware lest ye sow tares of dissension among men or plant thorns of doubt in pure and radiant hearts.

O ye beloved of the Lord! Commit not that which defileth the limpid stream of love or destroyeth the sweet fragrance of friendship. By the righteousness of the Lord! Ye were created to show love one to another and not perversity and rancor. Take pride not in love for yourselves but in love for your fellow-creatures. Glory not in love for your country, but in love for all mankind. Let your eye be chaste, your hand faithful, your tongue truthful and your heart enlightened.[310]

Bahá'u'lláh

Should Everyone Investigate the Bahá'í Faith?

The Bahá'í Faith is not just for Christians and Jews. It is for the ***entire*** human race. All sacred Scriptures have foretold the Advent of a great Redeemer who comes to unify the world and establish a glorious civilization:

All the...Books of God are adorned with His praise and extol His glory.[311]   Bahá'u'lláh

Every human being has a spiritual obligation to test the validity of Bahá'u'lláh's mission. Sometimes we make decisions based simply on unverified assumptions. Soon we learn the consequences. As a rule, the consequences come too late to repair the damage. We are told that every decision (good or bad) has only short-lived results except the ones that affect the state of our soul, the ones that determine our relationship with God. Such decisions must be taken more seriously than any others, yet most people take them very lightly, less seriously than the most trivial decisions of their lives, such as buying a toothbrush. They investigate the toothbrush but not the truth. Even if one chooses an unsuitable profession, it does not matter much, for death puts an end to everything except the spiritual state of the soul.

If we ignore God's guidance, our souls remain in despair and darkness. God's guidance is the light for our inner life.

> He that was hidden from the eyes of men is revealed, girded with sovereignty and power!... O ye that inhabit the heavens and the earth! There hath appeared what hath never previously appeared. He Who, from everlasting, had concealed His Face from the sight of creation is now come.[312]
> Bahá'u'lláh

> Seize the time, therefore, ere the glory of the divine springtime hath spent itself, and the Bird of Eternity ceased to warble its melody, that thy inner hearing may not be deprived of hearkening unto its call. This is My counsel unto thee and unto the beloved of God. Whosoever wisheth, let him turn thereunto; whosoever wisheth, let him turn away. God, verily, is independent of him and of that which he may see and witness.[313]
> Bahá'u'lláh

> And the Spirit and the bride say, Come. And let him that heareth say, Come. And let him that is athirst come. And whosoever will, let him take the water of life freely.
> Christ (Rev. 22:17)

All around us we find countless people whose companions are stress and distress, and whose partners are despair, confusion, fear, and loneliness. The tragedy is this: They are used to this life of quiet desperation and think that's the way it's supposed to be. As the prophet Joel predicted, "Yes, gladness has faded among the sons and daughters of the human race" (Joel 1:1-2). The world is sick and getting sicker by the hour. We are blessed with the gift of freedom. We can step aside and be mere observers of human suffering or step forward and play a positive role in the divine drama. The prophet Malachi predicted, "But to you who fear my name the Sun of Righteousness shall arise with healing in His wings" (Malachi 4:2). Bahá'ís believe that the Sun of Righteousness has dawned, and that His light offers eternal healing to the diseased soul of humanity:

> Witness how the world is being afflicted with a fresh calamity every day. Its tribulation is continually deepening...Its sickness is approaching the stage of utter hopelessness, inasmuch as the true Physician is debarred from administering the remedy, whilst unskilled practitioners are regarded with favor, and are accorded full freedom to act... The dust of sedition hath clouded the hearts of men, and blinded their eyes. Erelong, they will perceive the consequences of what their hands have wrought in the Day of God. Thus warneth you He Who is the All-Informed, as bidden by One Who is the Most Powerful, the Almighty.[314]
>
> Bahá'u'lláh

> The whole of mankind is in the grip of manifold ills. Strive, therefore, to save its life through the wholesome medicine which the almighty hand of the unerring Physician hath prepared.[315]
>
> Bahá'u'lláh

"A teacher of righteousness" has come with a new wine that intoxicates the soul. It is the time for rejoicing! "I am sending you grain, new wine and oil...rejoice in the Lord your God. For he has given you a teacher for righteousness" (Joel 2:19, 23). This is not the time for gloom and grief; even the trees of the forest are celebrating and singing for joy:

> Then all the trees of the forest will sing for joy; they will sing before the Lord, for He comes...
>
> Psalms 96:12-13

The dawn has broken, the Sun has risen. This is not the time of rest and repose:

> **O SON OF MAN!**
> Many a day hath passed over thee whilst thou hast busied thyself with thy fancies and idle imaginings. How long art thou to slumber on thy bed? Lift up thy head from slumber, for the Sun hath risen to the zenith, haply it may shine upon thee with the light of beauty.[316]   Bahá'u'lláh

Like the lightning, His light has spread to the farthest reaches of the earth. Why are people sleeping?

> ...don't let Him [the Redeemer of our time] find you sleeping.   Christ (Mark 13:36)

> Happy the man who stays awake [at the time of the Master's return]...   Christ (Rev. 16:15)

The world is filled with both *gloom* and *glory*. The choice is ours:

> Holy, holy, holy is the Lord of hosts [the Redeemer of our time]; the whole earth is full of His *glory*!   Isaiah 6:2

> Know thou of a certainty that the Day Star of Truth hath, in this Day, shed upon the world a radiance, the like of which bygone ages have

never witnessed. Let the light of His *glory*, O
people, shine upon you...[317]   Bahá'u'lláh

O SON OF MAN!
Ascend unto My heaven, that thou mayest obtain
the joy of reunion, and from the chalice of imperishable *glory* quaff the peerless wine.[318]
                                        Bahá'u'lláh

O MOVING FORM OF DUST!
I desire communion with thee, but thou wouldst
put no trust in Me. The sword of thy rebellion
hath felled the tree of thy hope. At all times I am
near unto thee, but thou art ever far from Me.
Imperishable *glory* I have chosen for thee, yet
boundless shame thou hast chosen for thyself.
While there is yet time, return, and lose not thy
chance.[319]   Bahá'u'lláh

A passenger reported being on a plane that was
ready for takeoff, when he heard a loud and persistent banging on the aircraft door. Finally the
crew checked, and found that the banging was
being caused by the captain of the plane, who had
somehow been locked out. Maybe that's what has
happened to our world today: We have locked out
the heavenly captain!

How Does One Become a Bahá'í?

Becoming a Bahá'í is as simple and yet as difficult
as acknowledging Bahá'u'lláh as God's Messenger
for this age, and making a commitment to practice
His laws and teachings. This does not require any
ceremonies.

The blessings, glories, and honors ordained for those who recognize the Redeemer of the age, especially at His dawning, are far beyond anything we can imagine. They will become manifest to us only in the next Kingdom.

> Whoso hath, in this Day, refused to allow the doubts and fancies of men to turn him away from Him Who is the Eternal Truth...to deter him from recognizing His Message, such a man will be regarded by God, the Lord of all men, as one of His mighty signs, and will be numbered among them *whose names have been inscribed by the Pen of the Most High in His Book*. Blessed is he that hath recognized the true stature of such a soul, that hath acknowledged its station, and discovered its virtues [emphasis added]...[320]
>
> Bahá'u'lláh

> But at that time your people—everyone *whose name is found written in the book*—will be delivered...Those who are wise will shine like the brightness of the heavens [emphasis added].
>
> Daniel 12:1-3

> Verily I say, this is the Day in which mankind can behold the Face, and hear the Voice, of the Promised One...It behoveth every man to blot out the trace of every idle word from the tablet of his heart, and to gaze, with an open and unbiased mind, on the signs of His Revelation, the proofs of His Mission, and the tokens of His glory.[321] Bahá'u'lláh

> Blessed the ear that hath heard and the tongue that hath borne witness and the eye that hath

seen and recognized the Lord Himself, in His great glory and majesty, invested with grandeur and dominion. Blessed are they that have attained His presence. Blessed the man who hath sought enlightenment from the Day-star of My Word. Blessed he who hath attired his head with the diadem of My love. Blessed is he who hath heard of My grief and hath arisen to aid Me among My people...Blessed is he who hath remained faithful to My Covenant, and whom the things of the world have not kept back from attaining My Court of holiness. Blessed is the man who hath detached himself from all else but Me, hath soared in the atmosphere of My love, hath gained admittance into My Kingdom, gazed upon My realms of glory, quaffed the living waters of My bounty, hath drunk his fill from the heavenly river of My loving providence...Verily, he is of Me. Upon him rest My mercy, My loving-kindness, My bounty and My glory.[322]   Bahá'u'lláh

O Lord of Hosts, my King and my God. Happy are those who dwell in thy house...   Psalms 84:4

Becoming a Bahá'í is as challenging as recognizing that Bahá'u'lláh is the Promised One of our age, and as consequential as coming to this far-reaching conclusion: His Word is the Word of God, and therefore must be trusted, honored, and obeyed.

In many countries, for the purpose of keeping records, the person who declares his or her faith in Bahá'u'lláh signs a card, requesting enrollment in the Bahá'í Faith. What happens if a person changes his or her mind after signing the card? All it takes is a letter to the Bahá'í National Office stating that one no longer believes in Bahá'u'lláh.

Faith is a matter of freedom, not force; a question of desire, not compulsion and coercion. God's Messengers teach us to love and respect all people, believers and non-believers alike. 'Abdu'l-Bahá states that we should never feel superior to anyone, including those who are not Bahá'ís. Even looking down on the worst sinners and deviants is evidence of pride. Pride masquerades in many robes and veils. It is always invisible and difficult to detect. We must always stand on guard against it.

A Few References for Continuing Your Investigation of the Bahá'í Faith

If you decide to remain watchful and continue your investigation, these are a few books you should definitely read:

- *Gleanings from the Writings of Bahá'u'lláh.*[323] This is the best compilation of the Writings of Bahá'u'lláh. It covers numerous topics and is not a book you will want to read through speedily. Reading it is essential, for we are asked to know a tree by its fruits. Scriptures of a faith are its first fruits.

- *The Proclamation of Bahá'u'lláh.*[324] This book contains Bahá'u'lláh's Epistles to political and religious leaders of His time. In these Epistles, He declares His Mission and invites the rulers of the earth to investigate His Message.

- *The Hidden Words of Bahá'u'lláh.*[325] This is a small book with beautiful and brief passages that summarize the spiritual teachings of all faiths. It is an inspirational book and shows—as do other works of Bahá'u'lláh—the distinction of divine words.

- *Bahá'í Prayers.*[326] This book contains many beautiful prayers from the Báb, Bahá'u'lláh, and 'Abdu'l-Bahá. Read it once and mark the prayers that appeal to you or that relate to your personal needs. Then recite the selected prayers every morning and evening. Persistent and whole-hearted praying is the key to the mansions of heaven. Without God's help we stand in the dark, confused and powerless.

- *The Glorious Journey to God.*[327] This book contains selections from sacred Scriptures of five great religions on the afterlife. This is an inspirational book on a topic of great concern to all human beings. It is the most comprehensive and reliable source of knowledge about the beyond.

- *The Hour of the Dawn.*[328] A brief history of the Advent of the Báb, a book that you can read in a day or two. It is a good beginning.

- *Day of Glory.*[329] A brief and simple account of the Advent of Bahá'u'lláh. This book is a sequel to *The Hour of the Dawn.*

- *Release the Sun.*[330] An expanded account of the Advent of the Báb and the dramatic events of His brief and amazing life.

- *Thief in the Night*.[331] This book lists biblical references to the Advents of the Báb and Bahá'u'lláh and is written in a simple and stimulating style. Once you start, you may not be able to put it down. I have known people who have read it straight through.

- *The Challenge of Bahá'u'lláh*.[332] This volume presents proofs of Bahá'u'lláh's divine distinction, especially His predictions.

- *I Shall Come Again*,[333] *Lord of Lords*,[334] and *King of Kings*.[335] These are the first three of six volumes I spent over 30 years writing. In these books you will find the most convincing evidence of the stations of the Báb and Bahá'u'lláh. You will be astonished by the number of detailed prophecies that designate the time of the Advents of the Báb and Bahá'u'lláh and much of the history of the Bahá'í Faith. If you intend to continue your investigation of the Bahá'í Faith and would like to receive a free copy of one of these books, please call 1-800-949-1863.

A few more books by this author:

- *Heaven's Most Glorious Gift*. This is a sequel to *One God, Many Faiths; One Garden, Many Flowers*.

- *Come Now, Let Us Reason Together*. This book responds to objections raised by a pastor against the Bahá'í Faith. It has a sequel: *Let Us Speak the Truth in Love*.

- *Seek and Ye Shall Find*. This book is addressed specifically to Christians. It invites them to arise and investigate the evidence Bahá'u'lláh presents for His divine Mission.

- *Destiny is a Choice*. This small book addresses these questions: Why do so many people fail to choose their destiny? Why do they leave this most fundamental of all choices in their lives to chance, to convenience, or to an unknown ancestor who lived and died long ago?

  Why do so many ignore, repress, postpone, forget, or avoid this most critical of all decisions?

  This book shows that the failure to address this question has been extremely costly, not only to individuals who have failed to take the responsibility, but also to the collective destiny of humankind throughout all ages.

- *On Wings of Destiny*. This is an introduction to the Bahá'í Faith and a sequel to *Destiny is a Choice*

- *Choosing Your Destiny*. This is a rather detailed introduction to the Bahá'í Faith.

- *The News Every Christian Should Know*. This small book invites Christians to investigate the Advent of their promised Redeemer—Bahá'u'lláh—who has come with a new name.

- *The Glory of the Son*. Before knowing the true evidence for another religion, we should know the true evidence for our own—the one on which we base our everlasting destiny. If we do not know why we believe in our own faith, how can we know why we should believe in another faith? *The Glory of the Son* offers a brief summary of all the reasons Jesus gave to substantiate His claim. This is a book every Christian should read.

It is also of value to those of Jewish faith who have a desire to know the evidence for the glory of the Son.

- *The Glory of the Father.* This is the sequel to *The Glory of the Son.* It applies the same standards to Bahá'u'lláh as *The Glory of the Son* applies to Jesus Christ.

- *A Messenger of Joy.* This small book of poetry presents a positive picture of the afterlife and removes the fear of dying.

A few books in progress by this author:

- *Does Your Fish Bowl Need Fresh Water?* This book covers topics that are the backbone of religion and faith, such as scientific evidence for the existence of God, the soul, and the afterlife. It portrays the design of creation (Why did God create the world the way it is?) and the purpose of suffering.

- *If There is One God, Why Are There so Many Religions?* This volume presents issues of concern to those who wish to investigate the Bahá'í Faith.

- *Hath the Hour Come?* This book is a call to Christians to awaken and investigate the Message of the Báb and Bahá'u'lláh. It offers many brief quotations from the Hebrew, Christian, and Bahá'í Scriptures to show their similarity, the oneness of their source, and their distinction. It demonstrates that the most conclusive evidence of religion is the miracle of words: its Scriptures, for God's Word is supremely distinct and distinguished.

Contents of the Next Volume

Heaven's Most Glorious Gift

Part I

Questions and Answers
About the Bahá'í Faith

Part II

An Invitation to Christians

A Guide to Self-Examination and Self-Knowledge

What Is Your Response to Bahá'u'lláh's Call?

A Few References for Continuing Your Investigation of the Bahá'í Faith

Part III

Quotations from the Writings of Bahá'u'lláh

Brief Quotations from Bahá'u'lláh's Epistle to the Pope and Religious Leaders of His Time

Brief Quotations from Bahá'u'lláh's Epistles Addressed to Political Leaders of the Earth

A Prayer from Bahá'u'lláh

Sources for Information and Literature

1. To receive information or a recorded message on the Bahá'í Faith, call: 1-800-228-6483.

2. Visit these Bahá'í Web Sites:
   - www.bahai.org
   - www.onecountry.org
   - www.bahai-library.org

3. Check the white and yellow phone pages for the Bahá'í Faith.

4. To receive free literature on the Bahá'í Faith, call us at: 1-800-949-1863.

5. To receive a free catalog of Bahá'í books or to order Bahá'í books in the United States, call Bahá'í Distribution Service: 1-800-999-9019, or write to:

   Bahá'í Distribution Service
   4703 Fulton Industrial Boulevard
   Atlanta, GA 30336-2017
   USA

Bahá'í National Centers in Some English Speaking Countries:

Alaska

13501 Brayton Drive
Anchorage, Alaska 99516
USA

Australia

Bahá'í Publications
173 Mona Vale Road
Ingleside, NSW 2101
Australia

Canada

7200 Leslie Street
Thornhill, Ontario
L3T 6L8 Canada

England

27 Rutland Gate
London SW7 1PD
United Kingdom

Hawaii

3264 Allan Place
Honolulu, Hawaii 96817
USA

India

Bahá'í House
5 Canning Road
Post Box 19
New Delhi 110 001
India

New Zealand

P.O. Box 21-551
Henderson 1231
Auckland
New Zealand

United States

536 Sheridan Road
Wilmette, IL 60091
USA

Notes and References

Preface

1. The anecdotes used in this book did not originate with this author. Sometimes they are quoted verbatim, but more often they have been edited, modified, summarized, or altered to fit the tone and the themes of this book. I express my deepest appreciation and debt to all creative thinkers who came up with the many memorable quotations and anecdotes cited in this book.

2. *The Promulgation of Universal Peace*, p. 63.

Questions and Answers About the Bahá'í Faith

1. *Tablets of Bahá'u'lláh*, pp. 78-79.
2. Motlagh, Hushidar. *I Shall Come Again*, Mt. Pleasant, MI: Global Perspective, 1992, p. 126.
3. Fox, Matthew. *The Coming of the Cosmic Christ*, Harper & Row, 1980, pp. 7-8.
4. Fox, Matthew. *The Coming of the Cosmic Christ*, Harper and Row, 1980, p. 2.
5. Fox, Matthew. *The Coming of the Cosmic Christ*, Harper and Row, 1980, p. 2.
6. Rawlings, Maurice S. M.D. *To Hell and Back*, Nashville: Thomas Nelson Publishers, 1993, p. 228.
7. *Selections from the Writings of the Báb*, p. 153.
8. *The Hidden Words of Bahá'u'lláh* (Arabic), no. 6.
9. *The Hidden Words of Bahá'u'lláh* (Arabic), no. 9.
10. *The Hidden Words of Bahá'u'lláh* (Persian), no. 32.

11. *Selections from the Writings of the Báb*, p. 23.

12. *Paris Talks*, p. 24.

13. *Selections from the Writings of the Báb*, p. 196.

14. *Selections from the Writings of the Báb*, pp. 105-106.

15. Stedman, Ray C. and James E. Denney. *God's Loving Word*, Grand Rapids, MI: Discovery House, 1993, p. 11.

16. *Tablets of Bahá'u'lláh*, p. 156.

17. *Selections from the Writings of the Báb*, p. 62.

18. *Gleanings from the Writings of Bahá'u'lláh*, p. 33.

19. *Epistle to the Son of the Wolf*, p. 59.

20. *Selections from the Writings of the Báb*, p. 112.

21. *The Kitáb-i-Íqán*, p. 53.

22. *Gleanings from the Writings of Bahá'u'lláh*, pp. 27-28.

23. *Gleanings from the Writings of Bahá'u'lláh*, p. 261

24. *Gleanings from the Writings of Bahá'u'lláh*, p. 59.

25. *The Kitáb-i-Íqán*, p. 100.

26. *Epistle to the Son of the Wolf*, p. 11.

27. Robbins, Anthony. *Awaken the Giant Within*, New York: Summit Books, 1991, p. 19

28. Bennett, William J. *The Index of Leading Cultural Indicators*, A Joint Publication of Empower America, The Heritage Foundation, and Free Congress Foundation, vol. 1, March 1993.

29. Bennett, William J. *The Index of Leading Cultural Indicators*, A Joint Publication of Empower America, The Heritage Foundation, and Free Congress Foundation, vol. 1, March 1993.

30. *Facts, Figures, and Quotes*, National Education Association.

31. *Awake!* April 8, 1994.

32. *Focus on the Family*, Newsletter, May 1993.

33. *NEA Newsletter*, 1994.

34. *Focus on the Family*, Newsletter, November 1994, p. 3.

35. *Focus on the Family*, Newsletter, November 1994, p. 3.

36. *Focus on the Family*, Newsletter, November 1994, p. 3.

37. *The Plain Truth*, November-December, 1994, p. 29.
38. *Obstetrics and Gynecology*, vol. 71, no. 4.
39. Carson, Robert C., James N. Butcher, and Susan Mineka, *Abnormal Psychology and Modern Life*, New York: Harper Collins College Publishers, 1996, p. 6.
40. *American Educator*, Winter 1994-95, p. 17.
41. *American Educator*, Winter 1994-95, p. 17.
42. Rawlings, Maurice S. M.D. *To Hell and Back*, Nashville: Thomas Nelson Publishers, 1993, p. 228.
43. Rawlings, Maurice S. M.D. *To Hell and Back*, Nashville: Thomas Nelson Publishers, 1993, pp. 227-228.
44. Prochnow Herbert V. *Speaker's & Toastmaster's Handbook*, Rocklin, CA: Prima Publishing, 1993, p. 241.
45. Colson, Charles. *The God of Stones and Spiders*, Wheaton, IL: Living Books, 1990, p. x.
46. *Breakpoint with Chuck Colson*, May 17, 1994, No. 40517.
47. *The Plain Truth*, November/December, 1994, p. 6.
48. *Tablets of Bahá'u'lláh*, p. 156.
49. *Selections from the Writings of the Báb*, p. 89.
50. *Selections from the Writings of the Báb*, pp. 88-89.
51. *The Bahá'í News*, May 1988, p. 2.
52. *Gleanings from the Writings of Bahá'u'lláh*, p. 146.
53. *Gleanings from the Writings of Bahá'u'lláh*, p. 5.
54. *The Kitáb-i-Íqán*, pp. 4-5.
55. *Selections from the Writings of the Báb*, p. 122.
56. *Some Answered Questions*, p. 101.
57. Hart, Michael H. *The 100, A Ranking of the Most Influential Persons in History*, New York: Citadel Press Book, 1989.
58. Kennedy, James. *Why I Believe*, Waco, TX: Word Books, 1980, p. 96.
59. *The Secret of Divine Civilization*, pp. 82-83.
60. *The Watchtower*, June 15, 1986, p. 13.
61. *The Kitáb-i-Íqán*, pp. 205-206.

62. *Gleanings from the Writings of Bahá'u'lláh*, p. 105.

63. *Selections from the Writings of the Báb*, p. 159.

64. *Selections from the Writings of the Báb*, p. 161.

65. *Selections from the Writings of the Báb*, p. 59.

66. *The Kitáb-i-Íqán*, p. 232.

67. *Selections from the Writings of the Báb*, p. 15.

68. *The Hidden Words of Bahá'u'lláh, (Arabic)*, no. 56.

69. *The Kitáb-i-Íqán*, p. 57.

70. *The Dawn-Breakers*, New York: Bahá'í Publishing Committee, 1953, p. 509.

71. *The Dawn-Breakers*, New York: Bahá'í Publishing Committee, 1953, p. 512.

72. *The Dawn-Breakers*, New York: Bahá'í Publishing Committee, 1953, p. 512.

73. *The Dawn-Breakers*, New York: Bahá'í Publishing Committee, 1953, p. 513.

74. *The Dawn-Breakers*, New York: Bahá'í Publishing Committee, 1953, p. 514.

75. *Selections from the Writings of the Báb*, p. 27.

76. *Selections from the Writings of the Báb*, pp. 27.

77. *Selections from the Writings of the Báb*, p. 166.

78. *Selections from the Writings of the Báb*, p. 156.

79. *The Beloved of the World* (translated from Persian), p. 184.

80. Ruhe David S. *Robe of Light*, Oxford: George Ronald, 1994, p. 21.

81. Marks, Geoffry W. *Call to Remembrance*, Wilmette, IL: Bahá'í Publishing Trust, 1992, p. 8.

82. Marks, Geoffry W. *Call to Remembrance*, Wilmette, IL: Bahá'í Publishing Trust, 1992, p. 11.

83. Marks, Geoffry W. *Call to Remembrance*, Wilmette, IL: Bahá'í Publishing Trust, 1992, pp. 11-12.

84. *Teacher Training Manual for Children's Classes, Age 6*, Columbia: Ruhi Institute, 1992, Section 3, pp. 7-8.

85. Marks, Geoffry W. *Call to Remembrance*, Wilmette, IL: Bahá'í Publishing Trust, 1992, pp. 14-15.

86. *Paris Talks*, p. 76.

87. *Epistle to the Son of the Wolf*, p. 21.

88. *Gleanings from the Writings of Bahá'u'lláh*, pp. 90-91.

89. *The Proclamation of Bahá'u'lláh*, p. 57.

90. *The Hidden Words of Bahá'u'lláh* (Persian), no. 52.

91. Marks, Geoffry W. *Call to Remembrance*, Wilmette, IL: Bahá'í Publishing Trust, 1992, pp. 166-167.

92. Momen, Wendi (ed.). *A Basic Bahá'í Dictionary*, Oxford: George Ronald, 1989, p. 155.

93. Momen, Wendi (ed.). *A Basic Bahá'í Dictionary*, Oxford: George Ronald, 1989, p. 155.

94. Marks, Geoffry W. *Call to Remembrance*, Wilmette, IL: Bahá'í Publishing Trust, 1992, p. 169.

95. *Paris Talks*, p. 79.

96. *Some Answered Questions*, 1981 ed., p. 35.

97. *The Proclamation of Bahá'u'lláh*, p. 19.

98. *The Proclamation of Bahá'u'lláh*, pp. 5-6.

99. Motlagh, Hushidar. *I Shall Come Again*, Mt. Pleasant, MI: Global Perspective, 1992, pp. 87-88.

100. Shoghi Effendi. *God Passes by*, Wilmette, IL: Bahá'í Publishing Trust, 1957, pp. 94-95.

101. *Tablets of Bahá'u'lláh*, p. 11.

102. *Tablets of Bahá'u'lláh*, p. 11.

103. *Gleanings from the Writings of Bahá'u'lláh*, p. 16.

104. *Gleanings from the Writings of Bahá'u'lláh*, p. 136.

105. *Gleanings from the Writings of Bahá'u'lláh*, p. 34.

106. *The Proclamation of Bahá'u'lláh*, pp. 111-112.

107. *Tablets of Bahá'u'lláh*, p. 11.

108. *Tablets of Bahá'u'lláh*, p. 13.

109. *Prayers and Meditations by Bahá'u'lláh*, pp. 103-104.

110. *Epistle to the Son of the Wolf*, p. 44.

111. *Selections from the Writings of the Báb*, p. 72.

112. *Selections from the Writings of the Báb*, p. 74.
113. *Selections from the Writings of the Báb*, p. 50.
114. *Selections from the Writings of the Báb*, p. 41.
115. *Selections from the Writings of the Báb*, p. 168.
116. *Selections from the Writings of the Báb*, p. 99.
117. *Selections from the Writings of the Báb*, p. 167.
118. *Selections from the Writings of the Báb*, p. 58.
119. Shoghi Effendi. *The World Order of Bahá'u'lláh*, Wilmette, IL: Bahá'í Publishing Trust, 1980, p. 113.
120. *Selections from the Writings of the Báb*, p. 72.
121. *Selections from the Writings of the Báb*, p. 71.
122. *Selections from the Writings of the Báb*, p. 159.
123. De Jong, Benjamin R. *Uncle Ben's Qutebook*, Grand Rapids, MI: Baker Book House, 1990, p. 53.
124. *Gleanings from the Writings of Bahá'u'lláh*, pp. 333-334.
125. *Gleanings from the Writings of Bahá'u'lláh*, pp. 78-79.
126. *Selections from the Writings of the Báb*, p. 126.
127. *Selections from the Writings of the Báb*, p. 159.
128. Covey, Stephen R. *The 7 Habits of Highly Effective People*, New York: Simon & Schuster, 1990, p. 29.
129. *The Promulgation of Universal Peace*, p. 198.
130. *Gleanings from the Writings of Bahá'u'lláh*, p. 214.
131. Shoghi Effendi. *The Promised Day Is Come*, Wilmette, IL: Bahá'í Publishing Committee, 1951, pp. 123-124.
132. *Bahá'í Prayers*, Wilmette, IL: Bahá'í Publishing Trust, 1991 edition, p. 204.
133. *Bahá'í Prayers*, Wilmette, IL: Bahá'í Publishing Trust, 1991 edition, p. 205.
134. *The Bahá'í Peace Program*, Wilmette, IL: Bahá'í Publishing Trust, 1967, p. 23.
135. Lample, Paul. *The Proofs of Bahá'u'lláh's Mission*, Riviera Beach, FL: Palabra Publications, pp. 5-6.
136. *Tablets of Bahá'u'lláh*, p. 157.

137. Anthony, Robert. *Total Self-Confidence*, New York: Berkley Books, 1984, pp. 3-4.

138. *Mankind's Search for God*, Brooklyn: Watchtower Bible and Tract Society of New York, Inc., 1990, pp. 8-10.

139. Arik, Abdullah. *Beyond Probability*, 1992, p. 2.

140. Dyer, Wayne. *You'll See It When You Believe It*, New York: Avon Books, 1989, pp. 164-165.

141. Dyer, Wayne. *You'll See It When You Believe It*, New York: Avon Books, 1989, p. 163.

142. Dyer, Wayne. *The Sky's the Limit*, New York: Pocket Books, 1980, p. 37.

143. *Paris Talks*, p. 136.

144. *The Bahá'í Faith and its World Community*, U.S. Bahá'í Office of Public Information, June 1992, p. 2.

145. *The Compilation of Compilations*, vol. 1, p. 393.

146. *The Compilation of Compilations*, vol. 1, p. 93.

147. *Gleanings from the Writings of Bahá'u'lláh*, p. 8.

148. Shoghi Effendi. *The Promised Day Is Come*, Wilmette, IL: Bahá'í Publishing Committee, 1951, p. 123.

149. Shoghi Effendi. *The Promised Day Is Come*, Wilmette, IL: Bahá'í Publishing Committee, 1951, p. 117.

150. Shoghi Effendi. *The Promised Day Is Come*, Wilmette, IL: Bahá'í Publishing Committee, 1951, p. 117.

151. Shoghi Effendi. *The Promised Day Is Come*, Wilmette, IL: Bahá'í Publishing Committee, 1951, p. 117.

152. *Selections from the Writings of the Báb*, p. 159.

153. *The Secret of Divine Civilization*, p. 109.

154. *The Compilation of Compilations,* vol. 2, p. 379.

155. Esslemont, J.E. *Bahá'u'lláh and the New Era*, Wilmette, IL: Bahá'í Publishing Trust, 1980, p. 147.

156. *The Hidden Words of Bahá'u'lláh* (Persian), no. 54.

157. *The Hidden Words of Bahá'u'lláh* (Persian), no. 49.

158. *Paris Talks*, pp. 153-154.

159. *Tablets of Bahá'u'lláh*, p. 26.

160. *Selections from the Writings of 'Abdu'l-Bahá*, p. 247.
161. *Selections from the Writings of 'Abdu'l-Bahá*, pp. 291-292.
162. *Gleanings from the Writings of Bahá'u'lláh*, p. 7.
163. *Gleanings from the Writings of Bahá'u'lláh*, p. 313.
164. *Gleanings from the Writings of Bahá'u'lláh*, pp. 333-334.
165. Shoghi Effendi. *The World Order of Bahá'u'lláh*, Wilmette, IL: Bahá'í Publishing Trust, 1980, pp. 203-204.
166. *Tablets of Bahá'u'lláh*, pp. 127-128.
167. *Selections from the Writings of 'Abdu'l-Bahá*, p. 127.
168. *The Hidden Words of Bahá'u'lláh* (Arabic), no. 68.
169. *The Hidden Words of Bahá'u'lláh* (Persian), no. 74.
170. *Gleanings from the Writings of Bahá'u'lláh*, p. 70.
171. *Selections from the Writings of 'Abdu'l-Bahá*, p. 117.
172. *Selections from the Writings of 'Abdu'l-Bahá*, p. 122.
173. *Bahá'í World Faith*, p. 364.
174. Paine, Mabel Hyde. *The Divine Art of Living*, Wilmette, IL: Bahá'í Publishing Trust, 1956, pp. 115-116.
175. *A Fortress For Well-Being*, Wilmette, IL: Bahá'í Publishing Trust, 1973, p. 15.
176. Shoghi Effendi. *The Advent of Divine Justice*, Wilmette, IL: Bahá'í Publishing Trust, 1984, p. 27.
177. *Tablets of Bahá'u'lláh*, p. 138.
178. *A Fortress For Well-Being*, Wilmette, IL: Bahá'í Publishing Trust, 1973, p. 16.
179. *A Fortress For Well-Being*, Wilmette, IL: Bahá'í Publishing Trust, 1973, p. 18.
180. *Selections from the Writings of 'Abdu'l-Bahá*, p. 129.
181. *Selections from the Writings of 'Abdu'l-Bahá*, p. 130.
182. *The Compilation of Compilations*, vol. 1, p. 269.
183. *The Compilation of Compilations*, vol. 1, pp. 266-267.
184. *The Promulgation of Universal Peace*, p. 181.
185. *The Kitáb-i-Íqán*, p. 184.

186. Elkind, David. *Young Children*, May 1987, p. 6.

187. *Paris Talks*, p. 51.

188. *Paris Talks*, p. 25.

189. *Paris Talks*, p. 24.

190. *The Hidden Words of Bahá'u'lláh* (Arabic), no. 12.

191. *The Hidden Words of Bahá'u'lláh* (Arabic), no. 11.

192. *The Hidden Words of Bahá'u'lláh* (Arabic), no. 12.

193. *The Hidden Words of Bahá'u'lláh* (Arabic), no. 13.

194. *Selections from the Writings of the Báb*, p. 162.

195. *Gleanings from the Writings of Bahá'u'lláh*, p. 250.

196. *The Bahá'í Faith and its World Community*, U.S. Bahá'í Office of Public Information, June 1992, p. 2.

197. "Fresh & Hopeful Models," *Herald of the South*, Oct.-Dec., 1994, pp. 8-9.

198. Barlett, Donald L. and James B. Steele. *America: What Went Wrong?* Kansas City: Andrews and McMeel, 1992, p. 4.

199. *The Bahá'í Faith and its World Community*, U.S. Bahá'í Office of Public Information, June 1992, p. 2.

200. *The Hidden Words of Bahá'u'lláh* (Persian), no. 81.

201. *Gleanings from the Writings of Bahá'u'lláh*, p. 265.

202. *Selections from the Writings of the Báb*, p. 154.

203. Esslemont, J. E. *Bahá'u'lláh and the New Era*, Wilmette, IL: Bahá'í Publishing Trust, 1980, p. 111.

204. Esslemont, J. E. *Bahá'u'lláh and the New Era*, Wilmette, IL: Bahá'í Publishing Trust, 1978, p. 116.

205. *Bahá'í Prayers*, Wilmette, IL: Bahá'í Publishing Trust, 1991 edition, p. 4.

206. *Bahá'í Prayers*, Wilmette, IL: Bahá'í Publishing Trust, 1991 edition, p. 28.

207. *Bahá'í Prayers*, Wilmette, IL: Bahá'í Publishing Trust, 1991 edition, p. 117.

208. *Bahá'í Prayers*, Wilmette, IL: Bahá'í Publishing Trust, 1991 edition, p. 152.

209. *Bahá'í Prayers*, Wilmette, IL: Bahá'í Publishing Trust, 1991 edition, pp. 153-154.

210. *Bahá'í Prayers*, Wilmette, IL: Bahá'í Publishing Trust, 1991 edition, p. 19.

211. *Bahá'í Prayers*, Wilmette, IL: Bahá'í Publishing Trust, 1991 edition, p. 87.

212. *Selections from the Writings of the Báb*, pp. 182-183.

213. *The Kitáb-i-Aqdas*, 1992, pp. 73-74.

214. *Selections from the Writings of the Báb*, p. 78.

215. Esslemont, J. E. *Bahá'u'lláh and the New Era*, Wilmette, IL: Bahá'í Publishing Trust, 1980, p. 116.

216. *World Order*, Summer 1978, vol. 12, p. 30.

217. *'Andalíb* (Persian), Fall 1993.

218. *The Kitáb-i-Íqán*, p. 205.

219. *Selections from the Writings of the Báb*, p. 26.

220. *Welcome to the Bahá'í House of Worship*, p. 5.

221. *The Promulgation of Universal Peace*, p. 15.

222. *The Promulgation of Universal Peace*, p. 8.

223. *The Hidden Words of Bahá'u'lláh* (Persian), no, 3.

224. *Selections from the Writings of 'Abdu'l-Bahá*, p. 280.

225. *Gleanings from the Writings of Bahá'u'lláh*, p. 33.

226. *The Promulgation of Universal Peace*, p. 218.

227. *The Promulgation of Universal Peace*, p. 218.

228. *Tablets of Bahá'u'lláh*, p. 71.

229. *Paris Talks*, p. 29.

230. *Selections from the Writings of 'Abdu'l-Bahá*, p. 245.

231. *The Promulgation of Universal Peace*, p. 93.

232. *Paris Talks*, p. 15.

233. *Selections from the Writings of 'Abdu'l-Bahá*, pp. 1-2.

234. *Tablets of Bahá'u'lláh*, p. 138.

235. *Gleanings from the Writings of Bahá'u'lláh*, p. 315.

236. *Gleanings from the Writings of Bahá'u'lláh*, p. 285.

237. *Selections from the Writings of the Báb*, p. 157.

238. *Selections from the Writings of the Báb*, p. 148.

239. Shoghi Effendi. *The World Order of Bahá'u'lláh*, Wilmette, IL: Bahá'í Publishing Trust, 1980, p. 108.

240. *The Hidden Words of Bahá'u'lláh* (Persian), no. 41.

241. Motlagh, Hushidar. *The Chalice of Immortality*, New Delhi, India: Bahá'í Publishing Trust, 1978, p. 114.

242. Ring, Kenneth. *Life at Death*, New York: Quill, 1982.

243. Moody, Raymond A. *Life After Life*, New York: Bantam Books, 1975, p. i.

244. Motlagh, Hushidar. *Unto Him Shall We Return*, Wilmette, IL: Bahá'í Publishing Trust, 1985, p. 6.

245. *Selections from the Writings of the Báb*, p. 161.

246. *The Hidden Words of Bahá'u'lláh* (Persian), no. 75.

247. Shoghi Effendi. *The Dispensation of Bahá'u'lláh*, Wilmette, IL: Bahá'í Publishing Committee, 1947, p. 15.

248. *The Kitáb-i-Íqán*, pp. 23-24.

249. *The Hidden Words of Bahá'u'lláh* (Persian), no. 21.

250. *The Kitáb-i-Íqán*, p. 252.

251. Motlagh, Hushidar. *A Messenger of Joy*, unpublished manuscript.

252. Motlagh, Hushidar. *The Glorious Journey to God*, Mt. Pleasant, MI: Global Perspective, 1994, p. 106.

253. *The Kitáb-i-Íqán*, pp. 256-257.

254. Covey, Stephen R. *The 7 Habits of Highly Effective People*, New York: Simon & Schuster, 1990, pp. 131-132.

255. *Bahá'í Prayers*, Wilmette, IL: Bahá'í Publishing Trust, 1991 edition, pp. 43-45.

256. Covey, Stephen R. *The 7 Habits of Highly Effective People*, New York: Simon & Schuster, 1990, p. 129.

257. *Gleanings from the Writings of Bahá'u'lláh*, p. 266.

258. *Gleanings from the Writings of Bahá'u'lláh*, p. 266.

259. *Gleanings from the Writings of Bahá'u'lláh*, p. 146.

260. *Bahá'í Prayers*, Wilmette, IL: Bahá'í Publishing Trust, 1991 edition, p. 152.

261. *Bahá'í Prayers*, Wilmette, IL: Bahá'í Publishing Trust, 1991 edition, p. 28.

262. *The Hidden Words of Bahá'u'lláh* (Arabic), no. 35.

263. *Epistle to the Son of the Wolf*, p. 57.

264. *Selections from the Writings of the Báb*, p. 145.

265. *The Kitáb-i-Íqán*, p. 120.

266. *Gleanings from the Writings of Bahá'u'lláh*, pp. 170-171.

267. *Selections from the Writings of the Báb*, p. 162.

268. *Selections from the Writings of the Báb*, p. 158.

269. *Epistle to the Son of the Wolf*, p. 133.

270. *Tablets of Bahá'u'lláh*, p. 189.

271. *The Hidden Words of Bahá'u'lláh* (Arabic), no. 6.

272. Shoghi Effendi. *The World Order of Bahá'u'lláh*, Wilmette, IL: Bahá'í Publishing Trust, 1980, p. 108.

273. *Gleanings from the Writings of Bahá'u'lláh*, pp. 9-10.

274. *Gleanings from the Writings of Bahá'u'lláh*, p. 161.

275. *Selections from the Writings of the Báb*, p. 147.

276. *Selections from the Writings of the Báb*, p. 77.

277. *Selections from the Writings of the Báb*, p. 79.

278. *Gleanings from the Writings of Bahá'u'lláh*, p. 321.

279. *Paris Talks*, p. 66.

280. Motlagh, Hushidar. *Unto Him Shall We Return*, Wilmette, IL: Bahá'í Publishing Trust, 1985, pp. 9-11.

281. *Selections from the Writings of the Báb*, p. 167.

282. *The Hidden Words of Bahá'u'lláh* (Persian), no. 7.

283. *Selections from the Writings of the Báb*, pp. 187-188.

284. *Selections from the Writings of the Báb*, p. 204.

285. *Selections from the Writings of the Báb*, pp. 95-96.

286. *Bahá'í Prayers*, Wilmette, IL: Bahá'í Publishing Trust, 1991 edition, pp. 45-46.

287. *Bahá'í Prayers*, Wilmette, IL: Bahá'í Publishing Trust, 1991 edition, pp. 46-47.

288. *Tablets of Bahá'u'lláh*, p. 52.

289. *Selections from the Writings of the Báb*, p. 98.

290. *Epistle to the Son of the Wolf*, p. 96.

291. *The Kitáb-i-Íqán*, p. 239.

292. *Gleanings from the Writings of Bahá'u'lláh*, p. 5.

293. *Selections from the Writings of the Báb*, p. 89.

294. *Tablets of Bahá'u'lláh*, p. 156.

295. *The Kitáb-i-Íqán*, p. 46.

296. *Tablets of Bahá'u'lláh*, p. 157.

297. *The Hidden Words of Bahá'u'lláh* (Persian), no. 36.

298. *Selections from the Writings of the Báb*, p. 103.

299. *The Promulgation of Universal Peace*, p. 148.

300. *The Kitáb-i-Íqán*, p. 3.

301. *Gleanings from the Writings of Bahá'u'lláh*, p. 136.

302. *The Hidden Words of Bahá'u'lláh* (Arabic), no. 59.

303. *The Hidden Words of Bahá'u'lláh* (Persian), no. 68.

304. *Paris Talks*, p. 138.

305. *The Hidden Words of Bahá'u'lláh* (Persian), no. 80.

306. *Gleanings from the Writings of Bahá'u'lláh*, p. 216.

307. *The Hidden Words of Bahá'u'lláh* (Arabic), no. 62.

308. Canfield, Jack and Mark Victor Hansen. *Chicken Soup for the Soul*, Deerfield Beach, FL: Health Communications, Inc. 1993, pp. 247-249.

309. Canfield, Jack and Mark Victor Hansen. *Chicken Soup for the Soul*, Deerfield Beach, FL: Health Communications, Inc., 1993, pp. 287-288.

310. *Tablets of Bahá'u'lláh*, p. 138.

311. *Tablets of Bahá'u'lláh*, p. 50.

312. *Gleanings from the Writings of Bahá'u'lláh*, p. 31.

313. *The Kitáb-i-Íqán*, p. 24.

314. *Gleanings from the Writings of Bahá'u'lláh*, pp. 39-40.

315. *Gleanings from the Writings of Bahá'u'lláh*, p. 81.

316. *The Hidden Words of Bahá'u'lláh* (Arabic), no. 62.

317. *Gleanings from the Writings of Bahá'u'lláh*, p. 319.

318. *The Hidden Words of Bahá'u'lláh* (Arabic), no. 61.

319. *The Hidden Words of Bahá'u'lláh* (Persian), no. 21.

320. Motlagh, Hushidar. *Unto Him Shall We Return* (a compilation), Wilmette, IL: Bahá'í Publishing Trust, 1985, p. 6.

321. *The Proclamation of Bahá'u'lláh*, p. 111.

322. *Tablets of Bahá'u'lláh*, pp. 16-17.

323. *Gleanings from the Writings of Bahá'u'lláh*, Wilmette, IL: Bahá'í Publishing Trust, 1983.

324. *The Proclamation of Bahá'u'lláh*, Haifa: Bahá'í World Centre, 1967.

325. *The Hidden Words of Bahá'u'lláh*, Wilmette, IL: Bahá'í Publishing Trust, 1970.

326. *Bahá'í Prayers*, Wilmette, IL: Bahá'í Publishing Trust, 1991.

327. Motlagh, Hushidar. *The Glorious Journey to God*, Mt. Pleasant, MI: Global Perspective, 1994.

328. Perkins, Mary. *The Hour of the Dawn*, Oxford: George Ronald, 1987.

329. Perkins, Mary. *Day of Glory*, Oxford: George Ronald, 1992.

330. Sears, William. *Release the Sun*, Wilmette, IL: Bahá'í Publishing Trust, 1995.

331. Sears, William. *Thief in the Night*, Oxford: George Ronald, 1987.

332. Matthew, Gary L. *The Challenge of Bahá'u'lláh*, Oxford: George Ronald, 1993.

333. Motlagh, Hushidar. *I Shall Come Again*, Mt. Pleasant, MI: Global Perspective, 1992.

334. Motlagh, Hushidar. *Lord of Lords*, Mt. Pleasant, MI: Global Perspective, 2000.

335. Motlagh, Hushidar. *King of Kings*, Mt. Pleasant, MI: Global Perspective, 2000.

We invite you to embark on a spiritual journey that will lead you to your heavenly hope.

We invite you to examine the Bahá'í pattern for a new world civilization.

We invite you to discover how effectively the Bahá'í Faith resolves our persistent social problems, how it strengthens family bonds, inspires high moral standards, and brings back the love of God to the heart of humanity.

We invite you to see God's magnificent plan for your own destiny and that of humankind for the next thousand years and more.

One God, Many Faiths will lift you above the threatening and thundering clouds of grief and gloom and show you a new Sun rising quietly with blazing beauty and splendor.